The Hidden Key Orgasm Reveals

Living a Blissful Life

AnnaMarie Antoski

ISBN-13: 978-0-9868844-0-5

DEDICATION

To my loving mate Jamie, in appreciation for your expanding unconditional love and support through all the years.

CONTENTS

ACKNOWLEDGMENTS

To all who have been my teachers which is every single being I have encountered in the past, present and future because in one way or another it has always been for a purposeful reason. It has helped me evolve to knowing more about myself and the nature of reality through every encounter.

I am most appreciative of Love, that all of us are created from, Infinite Love

CHAPTER 1

EXPANDING THE ORGASMIC STATE

I find it so incredibly amazing that something we experience for just a few seconds or minutes may hold the hidden key of the genuine nature of reality. Intertwined with expanded knowledge of the infinite wisdom of the most loving and powerful way to live our lives. All of this locked in a fantastic place, never to be lost, yet revealing it's secrets when we get into the experience of sexual pleasure and let go to experience orgasm.

The experience of orgasm that feels so challenging to describe in words of stirred emotions into feelings of heavenly bliss of ecstasy as the closest meaning to describe it. Yet that feeling is so fleeting for such a small amount of time in our space that we are constantly searching in any way possible to have that feeling repetitiously. That heavenly feeling only seems to last for a little bit and then it is gone until the next time, no wonder we love it so much and desire to always return to it.

It is so magnificent how orgasm is experienced for such a short time and yet has the most ultimate highest feeling. An experience of being so powerful in that small momentum of time to capture our hearts infinitely. What an impression it leaves us with and for an exuberant reason too.

The reason it leaves such an impression on us so simply and plainly shows that there is a greater reason for orgasm then just a pleasurable fleeting moment when we have sex. Have you also noticed that you really do not have to actually love someone to have sex and that orgasmic feeling? It became a popular statement in the past that instead of referring to having sex that we should refer to it as making love. However we know through experience that we do not have to love someone to experience making love to feel the spectacular experience of orgasm. We can also be that love being to create living an orgasmic life.

When we come to realize that we do not need another person to experience orgasm either, we can also enjoy the experience by our self and without all those old notions of guilt that once brought all those tainted attachments.

So really what does love or sex have to do with orgasm?

It all depends on what meaning we individually give to love or sex, and most of these definitions of beliefs are a result of the limited memories of consciousness. Pure genuine love that is felt in the orgasmic moment is a love that has no ego or limited personality of judgments contained in it. Orgasm is the genuine feeling we receive from the letting go into the ecstatic feeling that allows us to go further to experience its magical, magnificent state we are in for that moment that we are in it.

Orgasm is the hidden key to open our conscious awareness into a feeling, a state of being to remind us where we came from originally to begin with and expand on it. It is actually there for a purposeful universal reason then just a pleasure to experience and feel through any sexual pathway to get to that letting go feeling experience.

If you have already come to know that pure genuine love is the glue that holds everything together including ourselves, our planet, our universe and all universes, everything. That love has no conditions, no limits, no judgments, no comparisons, orgasmic love is allowing, accepting, freedom, and infinitely expanding unity. To realize that this love is not the same love most individuals live on a daily basis in relationships and commitments of the ego. This infinite love is our true selves, our true being, our true connection to everything and everyone, our true connection to the infinite creator.

Orgasm is there for a higher purpose!

Not just to get there from having sex, not just for a fleeting few moments of ecstasy, not for just a reserved few, not just for copulating either. The fleeting orgasmic moments are to capture our hearts and souls to trigger our selves to go further, to find the hidden key that reveals it's infinite secrets. By desiring more, to go further to know that it is our true natural feeling to be in all of the time.

It is where the purest, genuine sense of LOVE really is in that state of being, where we experience heaven, bliss, ecstasy, it is all intertwined, connectedly woven. The limiting ego mind has tainted love to be in many flavors contained of judgments and descriptive meanings of attachments that have nothing to do what real love, the love of the One Infinite Source Creator.

Once we get passed those limiting conditional memories, those stagnating beliefs that have kept us feeling like prisoners and victims for too long. It's the dogma of love being only shared with one, your partner, when we can see signs of infidelity everywhere, so we must ask for what purpose is this occurring? Yet we love our parents, siblings, children, friends, lovers, pets and so on, altering love to associate and separate a different frame work. Limited mindedness of humanity tried to box love into frames that only left love limited and attached with beliefs of judgments that only keeps boxing it in more, when love is free and expanding.

Thoughts and ideas valued hypnotically to condition humanity, dictating what have become beliefs that you can love your partner but it's a judgment if you love another by sexual intercourse. There are so many unique yet conditional ideas that most use to define pure infinite love as limiting, a result of old worn out conditional beliefs that were taught from ego love.

Limiting judgmental beliefs imply a ruled structure that you can love others but just do not have any sexual intercourse with them or it gets twisted. As if to believe that its okay to love another other then your partner even to the point of foreplay but if it comes to intercourse then you broke the covenant, so to speak. Or whatever limiting values you have come to attach to believe in any rules that dictates you away from unified infinite love.

Now just take a closer look at these structured limited beliefs that are trying to present themselves as rules and regulations to infinite love. It can really sound insane to create all these specific rules and regulations to love and how it should be dictated. How much free will or freedom do you find in it? Not much because all those rules are limiting, boxing us in and lack any freedom or free will that orgasmic heavenly genuine love is showing us .

So for starters we must move beyond the limited ego mind to know the Source of our Infinite Creator to expand our consciousness into our physical to comprehend to know some wisdom about infinite love. And those fleeting orgasmic moments can reveal so much to our selves of how to go beyond the old conditional rules that are becoming to not make sense.

As we evolve into the opportunity to allow orgasm's hidden key to reveal and show us it's true source, as we expand to move into real genuine infinite love to be known.

We must let go of all the limiting attachments that we have unconsciously attached to pure orgasmic love. When we know that love is an expression of the One Infinite Source Creator of Creations, then we also know that expression comes all free will. That means no conditions, no in that judgments and no rules to regulate something that is unlimited and infinite.

Lack, limitations, rules, judgments, victims, being not responsible for our own reality, is really being out of harmony of the flow of infinite pure love.

When you are in the release and the letting go to experience orgasm, are you doing any of the limited thinking?

I am quite sure you are answering a big No to that question! As we know to be in that orgasmic state you are too blissful even for that moment to be able to think of anything other then the state of bliss you are in. We can't even experience orgasm unless we are in that void infinitely magical state.

Through the act of foreplay we can be thinking of something other then what we are actually doing and if we are not focused by being in the void momentum of our foreplay then we will still be in the altered ego state. That would mean you are not fully focused a hundred percent of your attention in the foreplay, however when you do get focused into the void of foreplay is where you find the hidden key that unlocks the infinite wisdom to get to the orgasmic experience. And when the release of orgasm comes, there is no thought, just that tantalizing moment of bliss, that void of eternalness, that uplifting feeling that takes you to the highest void of ecstasy.

Does it matter how we got there?

No, there are multiple ways of getting there, just as there are multiple ways of traveling to a destination. Just as we have choices to walk, use a vehicle, bus, train or a plane to travel to destinations is the same as varieties of choices to take us to orgasm, it is not dependant on just one way.

Whether we travel to get there through foreplay with another or by your own self, or in doing anything that time just flies by. It is still the arrival, the experience. It is the thoughts you choose to think about what you are doing that allows you to get there or not.

Just as your arrival to a destination is analogous to your destination experience of orgasm, regardless how you get there.

Let's comprehend this wisdom to realize that orgasm is the hidden key to bringing that ecstasy feeling into our daily lives, what is referred to as heavenly bliss, that magical state.

We will use the analogy of orgasm as the destination

So let us imagine that you picked a trip to a destination and your desire is to experience the different cultures or just as a get away, its still for the joy of the experience.

You choose your method of travel, let's say it's a plane. So the plane is similar to foreplay or any other choice you use that is going to transport you, your being to your destination of the trip, just as the destination of orgasm.

You either enjoy the traveling the same way you would get to any destination of a physical location or orgasms experience. Or if you did not enjoy your travel or way of transportation, the desire for your destination allowed you to make the best of it. It can be the same way with orgasm as the destination and foreplay as the transportation to get you to the end result or the orgasmic experience.

If you did not want sex, you do not get into the focus of foreplay it would be similar to not using the transportation to take you to your destination. If you cancelled your trip it would be the same as canceling the experience of orgasm. However when you decided to finally enjoy it and go with it, you will arrive at your destination or orgasm.

If you did not, it is just delayed, eventually you will get to the experience of orgasm, the destination awaits you when you are ready, it will always be there in any future time.

Expanding Orgasm into Daily Living

Now let's expand on the analogy that if you decided to get off the plane you then can enjoy your experiences at the destination. However if you did not get off the plane you miss out on the rest of the trip.

Most of us would agree that the best part of the trip is enjoying the experience once arriving at the destination that you have traveled to. But if you choose not to get off the plane then you would land up back at your starting point eventually in the return flight without experiencing the rest of the trip, instead of getting off the plane when it landed. That would be the same as arriving at orgasm for a few fleeting moments and then not getting off the plane, not expanding the orgasmic feelings any longer or into anything else. This makes sense right?

It is coming to the realized key of wisdom that orgasm is there in an enticing way to expand on and that is a clue for the reason that it leaves such a wild, magical and heavenly ecstasy impression to begin with.

When we come down from that blissful heavenly experience we feel from orgasm is when thoughts return, back to reality, back to altering from orgasmic bliss and back to ego limited thoughts.

So the proof is in the orgasm. The proof is in the state you are in for the time that you are in that magical void state. That state is a reminder to peak your curiosity to know more about it. To realize that orgasm is there for a very exuberant universal reason of how we can feel regularly through everything we do. Not to just arrive at that destined state of experience with such intense feelings and never get off the plane. Or only experience it when we have sex, but to love that orgasmic feeling and desire to feel it more and more in everything we do.

I believe it is triggering us to know more of how our life can be lived by expanding the orgasmic state, from our Loving Infinite Source to our real true selves in everything we do.

That would move us from experiences of being stressed out that leads us perpetually to depression, those feelings that many think we have no control over it. As a result these beliefs leads us to trying to fill ourselves with everything and anything to get us to that ecstatic orgasmic state again.

To expand and stay in that orgasmic blissful state of being all through the day we must work on it daily, by being aware and observing the thoughts we are choosing.

If any thoughts we are choosing are not creating us to feel good emotions, then all we need to do is pick thoughts that can bring us to better feeling thoughts. It is taking this into daily practice as much as we possibly can to start to feel the differences of the old thinking to the better feeling thinking.

We could use descriptions of heaven and hell or bliss and stress, what would you prefer? It all depends on what we think about anything and everything. These ponderings brought into practice will bring about the variety of feelings to know the differences and keep us desiring the orgasmic blissful state into more and more, just because it feels so blissfully good.

This may be one powerfully great purposeful reason to be in the physical plane of existence to realize what its like to live heavenly through the feeling of orgasm. The hidden key on earth to reveal through our physical bodies to have the experience to desire it to be the catalyst for living our life.

To expand that same experience in everything we do in every way. Then we have arrived at the destination of what many refer to as heaven on earth and loved it so much that we decided to live there and never go back to the old ways.

CHAPTER 2

\ \ \ \ \ \ \ \ \ \ \ \ \ \ \ \ \ \ \ \

MAGIC AND MYSTERY REVEALED

One thing we know for absolute is that orgasm captures and feels magically mysterious while we are in orgasm's experience. Magical for many of us may have a spell bounding mysterious vibration to it because of the associations that enchantment brings.

Magic has an alluring mystery we perceive of being able to do something extraordinaire and mysterious for most individuals of something so out of the ordinary. Yet to some future beings what appears magical and mysterious to us may be normal every day reality for them because they have mastered to do all the time.

How prehistoric are we?

We have our valued conditions and superstition beliefs that perpetuate our limitations and stagnate ourselves from our empowering capabilities. Yet magic is still mysterious to the limited minds who still have limited thoughts attached to it to describe its meaning. They may also perceive through trickery to wondering if any magical thing is true because that perception is not trusting or realizing our true power of abilities we do have available to us.

When we unveil any old beliefs with newer expanding evolved ones there is always a lapse for awhile until the majority finally start to go along with it. Just as believing the world was flat at one time.

Orgasm so ecstatically shows us the feelings that go with orgasm such as bliss, ecstasy, heaven, magical, mystery, of the highest feeling of pleasure and are sparks to get us to expand into more of what the future can offer us.

So just as citizens finally let go of the belief that the world was still flat when Columbus explored to prove the world was round and they would not fall off the edge through their travels as many limited people believed. This is similar to what orgasm is trying to reveal it's hidden key to show us of our true real infinite selves. Of what real infinite love really is and what creation and universes and other worlds are all about. Leading us to ponder into the journey further to wonder about the key of orgasm to follow the seemingly magical mysterious path to follow, then the magic and mysteries will be revealed.

Allowing us to delve into the realm of possibilities that are infinite and probable when we evolve out of the old limiting thinking to get to know God or the Infinite Source. The one Creator of All Source, which is Source of Love of all possibilities and no conditions, referred to as unconditional love. Where everything is not only possible but fun and exciting, heavenly, stretching us further and further through each leap to feel a bit more comfortable for the next leap.

Allowing Orgasm to Reveal the Mysteries

Orgasm can reveal to us to see through the illusions of mystery because it sparks the desire to ignite, to want it more and know more. To expand from that one powerful spark that if we follow it's lead will guide us into the most wonderful world of our future and to start experiencing it right now.

Magic and mystery are all about unveiling it's true workings, melting away the illusions that made something appear magical or mysterious. When we look behind the veil we see something even more magically mysterious that we may have thought in our past. It will releases us from the old way of perceiving as tricks and to actually know what appears as mysterious.

Getting to know the appearing mysterious unknown is very powerful when we come to know what's revealed behind the mystery without the tricks of the ego altered thinking that limits our perception. We then can not only see past the unbelievable to believe, we expand further into the knowing and that knowing becomes wisdom when we experience making any unknown know for ourselves.

When we experience to see through these illusions, we evolve to expanded our understanding of what seemed mystical was just evolved information to know. Things that may have threatened us with fearful thoughts that limit our beliefs in the impossibilities become melted down to allow us to expand into more knowing of its truths.

It is only our limited thinking that creates fear in us that the possibility of ESP abilities as telepathy, teleporting, remote viewing, telekinesis, levitation and melting metal to become in its energetic state of fluidity. And there is so much more to explore.

It is when we get to know that the illusion associated to magic and mystery becomes of our own wisdom.

The wisdom of knowing is expanded when we know that everything is energy. That means our bodies are energy, our thoughts are energy, all object are energy, everything. Then we become to comprehend to understand that we do affect everything because we are one and the same, just in different vibration variables of frequencies. Which quantum physics is showing us what ancient masters have also taught which is showing us what we really are in these physical bodies in this physical planet of earth. That we are infinite spiritual beings in physical bodies on the plane of earthly existence, learning to work our energy deliberately with physical matter to manipulate it into what we desire.

It is orgasm that unlocks that key to reminding us of this wisdom. So lets continue to unveil the mysteries of orgasm.

When we want to know that means we have the key. When we ponder to wonder more then we use the key to opening the door slightly. When we know we are then inside, mystery is revealed through orgasm.

CHAPTER 3

\ \

ONE STATE OF BEING IS ALL IT TAKES

Let us expand our minds without our ego judgments to reveal some real ideas about addictions. To realize how it may be potentially needed to let go of all the negative attachments of what addiction presently may hold. And how important this realization may be because pleasure, joy, fun, a relaxed state of peaceful bliss is of the infinite love energy. Yet so much conditional energy concerning beliefs of addiction are not loving but the opposite of love that is based in fear energy.

Pleasure and orgasm are both of a high vibration and the reason that we feel heavenly pleasure and want to have more and more of something and to perpetually return to having more. So to have more and more is really a good thing not a bad thing, even if anyone tries to dictate through their suggestions from their beliefs to imply it not to be.

To have more is to experience more pleasure and what is pleasure? Pleasure is a God like quality, just add an "o" to God and we get the word Good, that's quite an easy hidden meaning sign to see through.

So let us really soak in this notion of the idea that yes to have pleasure from more is good, Godlike. And what do we know about our universe now, it is continuously expanding and expanding is more and more, not less and less. Addictions have the attachment of ideas from beliefs that more is not good, so have less until none, until all of our pleasures are gone and then we can become numb and depressed.

So let us go with more is good and godlike and expands into more and more pleasure to expand to feeling more and more heavenly from what orgasm allows us to experience for that short moment in time. Let us go back to the feeling we feel, the state we are in when we have come to letting go and feeling the experience of orgasm. The orgasmic experience is of pure joy, blissful, magical, mysterious, heavenly, ecstasy, pleasurable and leaves us with wanting more of it because it feels so godlike of a feeling of reality for that moment in time.

It feels like space as we know it and time as we know it seem to collapse into a state of Infinity for a few moments. Multiple orgasms is the experience of expanding that ecstasy even longer.

If you have not experienced multiple orgasms then it is an ecstatic experience still awaiting for you to still experience.

How do you get there?

It is quite simple but may not be that easy if your beliefs get in the way, but just by the pureness of desiring it and then trusting it by knowing which leads you to expecting it. However remember and the purpose of this book is to get you to experiencing orgasmic bliss on a minutely daily base, bringing orgasmic bliss from the future into your present reality as much as you possibly can. That means to be able to feel orgasmic with everything all through the day.

Space and Time Collapse into Eternity

When we come to the realization to know we are in space using time, its profound. Knowing we are Source, Spirit experiencing ourselves in human form in a reality of space that we experience, time that is expanding for the experience of it.

Now let us think about time. Time when we are referring to it as linear perceptions, that is how many individuals are living it, by clocks, schedules, calendars and so on. That is linear time, however the real infinite of consciousness reality of time its not linear even in physical. Because we can experience time flying when we are having fun and time feeling to go by so slowly if we are not having a good time. So linear time and no time in space are simultaneously interwoven throughout our days. And is in conjunction to what we are doing that keeps us boxed into linear time for most of our time of our days.

If we are truly doing what we love then our linear perception of how we experience time may not be so structured with schedules of the clock and calendars. The point here is getting to know the differences, the varieties of contrast of how flexible time really is in space.

Space seems to be infinite and we measure it by using time as a tool to experience and work around in it. Our physical senses create assumptions to comprehend through our physical sensory of reality through our perceptions. We perceive physical solidness of time in space. So it appears to me that our perception of time can be what expands us in space, and orgasm is timeless in infinite space, as we are in the orgasmic state of being.

So the sparks of non linear, timelessness is always sparking and expanding, intermingling into our solidness of physical. It allows us to experience more of our true self and true nature of reality, just as orgasm can do. It is in that orgasmic state that there is no time, no space, just heavenly bliss that seems to spark us for a moment into infinity.

Even though we have a challenge with understanding infinity, the infinite state of being, except for the feeling of heavenly ecstasy we experience. Or if we are doing something we love to do we are in that timeless space of infinity too.

In orgasm we only experience sparks of it but enough to entice us to not only to want more of the experience but to also find ways to expand the experience to have more and more of it.

Peaking into the Doorway of Infinity through Orgasm

It is like peaking into a doorway of infinity that sparks our desire with such passionate inspiration for more of it.

The so called label of addiction also brings us to the same states in different ways as another tool to get us there too. That is the reason I choose to not label judgments of conditioned beliefs to any addiction because if something is pleasurable for me, that's all the meaning I want it to be, pure joy. Even if the pleasure memory of an addiction was created from something at the time in my past when a certain addiction started for me and I was not aware of neutral meaning in everything.

I know now that I have the free will to transform everything to be of a higher potential. In other words it will work to my own advantage of a divine nature for my self and my body. That is what free will, joy, present now moments, neutral meaning and heaven on earth to me is all about. To enjoy now not later or feel guilty for an addiction I have whether its coffee, cigarettes, whatever it is doesn't matter. I just feel there is no reason or benefit at all in using something and then adding guilt beliefs to it. If we are going to do whatever the addiction is we might as well associate a belief of benefit and pleasure to it. For the most important reason being the body and brain is always on command to our thoughts that become beliefs and are creating our body from those commands of thoughts whether we are aware of it or not.

Whatever it is I am doing I perceive it as a pleasure experience in this present moment for me, then it is a pleasure and that is it. Which means it is my choice and I choose not to give any attached definitions to mean anything that would give it a negative meaning. Except the pleasurable orgasmic feeling of experiences of infinity it gives or allows me to be in. There is no good or bad about anything.

I smoke, it's not good or bad, healthy or unhealthy for me, it is just a pleasure with no conditions or judgments. I brought it back to a neutral state which is an enjoyment without attached beliefs of any kind but the pleasurable orgasmic feeling I experience. That way my body is not reacting to create any disease from attaching negative thoughts of programs to create negative results.

It just Is what It Is, Neutral.

What we define whatever anything is to be.

If we're consciously aware we have the advantage to define anything for it's highest benefit. If we are not choosing to be consciously aware then automatic programs of past memories will give it the definition and command instead.

The body will only respond to what we believe in our idea's of the meaning to define everything. Over 70 trillion body cells that are taking commands all of the time from the meaning we give to everything.

There are individuals throughout the world who drink poison and it does not affect their body at all. They have taken the idea of poison to a neutral orgasmic state of nothingness and created beliefs that it will not affect them at all, and it does not.

So it is when we remove all ideas of thoughts to addictions that our power returns, the illusions dissolve, the truth is unveiled, we are godlike in our evolution to returning to the real love, creators heavenly bliss in all things. That one state is all it takes to sustain the orgasmic ride of living our life blissfully.

We give meaning to everything.

It is up to our own self and when we know it we become sovereign beings onto our own self allowing our infinite self to come through. We are creating reality and our body's reality from what we desire it to become and do it from what we think about everything that becomes our belief about it.

Look at all the power you get when you take yourself back from all those conditions or conditionings that created so many false beliefs to begin with from past memories.

When we come to realize all of this about addiction we come to realize that it really is one state of being to be in regardless of any limited conditioned beliefs.

The Orgasmic State is pleasure and if we stay in that pleasurable state and create beliefs to support it by valuing the orgasmic state we expand it into more continuously. Then that is the experience and benefits we are going to have. The pleasurable orgasmic state, heaven on earth in everything we think or do state of being.

Now from the experience of time in space collapsing into infinity is the key that orgasm allows us to experience is also showing us that we can do this with everything. This key that unlocks our remembering of our ecstatic empowerment of feeling from those brief glimpses sparking to want more to sustain the momentum to use it with everything.

Coffee and so called junk food can be perceived in the comparison as what once was thought that junk DNA was useless. Then they found out it what was thought to be junk DNA is there for many reason, to evolve, activate more empowerment in ourselves.

Nothing is useless ... everything is there for a reason. Junk food is only perceived as no good and unhealthy if you put those constricted limited thought ideas to believe it which will create it to be that way for you. Just as the individuals who neutralized their beliefs with poison can be done with junk food. So if we believe there is a higher purposeful reason for everything then we take that to consider everything not just a few things. When we know especially from experience that we can neutralize our beliefs about everything by bringing it to the nothing state and then recreate it to our own pleasurable beneficial benefits.

Would it not be more creative to create a beneficial meaning to define junk food? Instead of creating something unbeneficial as most do, instead create a program that the body would respond to junk food to be of a nutritional value for your body. Giving a potential program so the body will respond and sustain your evolving sovereignty. Then junk food would be used for a greater and higher purpose. To enjoy freely whenever you want and it automatically transforms to nutritional energy whenever you eat it.

And that is exactly what I have been doing for years. You would keep yourself in that one pleasurable orgasmic state when eating junk food and your body will treat it that way, nutritionally good for you. The body doesn't know the difference, it follows the beliefs that program you brain by your thoughts about everything and then on command creates the body to create it that way.

Sure we can do what the normal do, just don't eat it, but then how would we ever know if all the ancient wisdom was true or not? For myself I enjoy these opportunities to experiment with so that I know for my myself of it's validity that it works this way. And it should because we are creators creating our reality and we really do get to choose, it's our divine nature of our infinite heritage. If we bring our state of being back into our infinite orgasmic state we are then using our empowering ability of creating reality consciously.

So when I think of junk food, I think of it as healthy glucose for my brain and body. Junk food is neutral until I give it meaning and the meaning I give is most powerful when I choose the meaning to be of the best potential for myself.

It is not what you eat that's matters, it is what you think about what you eat that gives your brain and body the commands that becomes what you then physically perceive. Our body is what we think it to be, constantly we are doing it all the time but most are not aware of this wisdom.

This works the same way for everything and anything.

It is the state of being we are in that will be creating our body and reality.

We can go on endlessly about redefining everything that we gave past unbeneficial meaning to just by desiring to do so. We can do it by using our desires as our bridge to change anything that's not of our highest benefits. It will take knowing that everything is always infinitely evolving and expanding that includes ourselves too. So whether it is cell phones, chocolate, cigarettes or drugs, it does not matter. It will always be the thoughts we choose about everything that creates the beliefs about anything that will be our creation.

So it is great to remind yourself often that everything is neutral, it is the meaning that you give it to define it as a belief of thoughts that will have the reaction from that meaning. It will be the state you choose to be in, we only need one state to be in and that's the orgasmic state because that will transform everything to be beneficially divine with blissful experiences as a result. We can refer to it as the orgasmic state of being.

Whether we deny we are Creators or know it will create all the difference. Orgasm is the key to being an ecstatic creative creator, the way we were meant to be.

We are all gods or creator's looking back at ourselves and for many individuals they just have not realized it yet. We all can when we are ready to evolve to that wisdom, it will always be there to know, just as orgasm is there to know of a greater higher divine universal purpose too. We are evolving and growing into more expansive creators with every old conditioning to break through. Melting away and putting orgasmic ideas of meanings into our daily lives into everything we objectify does change everything. **Where did it all evolve from in the first place?** That simple fleeting momentum of time in space collapsing to know that heaven may just be what was hidden away in orgasm all this time. Sparking us to go further to know more to bring it into everything in our daily lives so it can heal, empower everything for us. Which brings us to the next chapter to have the more of it by keeping ourselves to expand as the universe does into the present now all the time through orgasmic bliss.

CHAPTER 4

\ \ \ \ \ \ \ \ \ \ \ \ \ \ \ \

REVELATIONS OF MORE

Let's take a closer look at the definition of more.

More is to expand, go further, add to, multiply and so on. Our universe is expanding not decreasing. Quantum physics is showing us proof that we are expanding into needing to realize that there are infinite dimensions not just three, four, five or eleven. Most of us on this expanding journey of remembering we are in physical bodies but as an extension of an infinite self or source creator. More and more planets are being discovered as our instruments become more powerful through technical advances. Cells in petri dishes multiply. Bacteria, which was one of the first creations to multiply, sustain expanding and survival from the beginning of our planet's creation. The planets population is expanding. More of the population of this planets limited consciousness is expanding into choosing thoughts from higher consciousness. So all of this more that we observe, that is expanding in everything is definitely for good reasons, wouldn't you think?

Except when it comes to the idea of addictions

Addiction was created to describe in referral to something that we continuously want because we just cannot seem to get enough of it. It has been taught that what we are trying to do with addictions is fill ourselves up with everything externally to get us to what our natural creator's state really is, that orgasmic feeling.

All these teaching of external pleasures to be only a substitute for our infinite source of self that we are not feeling naturally on our own. So instead we are using the other things to do what can be felt naturally if we just would give up the other external things long enough. So addiction was created by labeling it as a meaning to describe an altered ego state which is fear energy.

The only thing I find negative and resistant to this idea is that by creating these labeled states for addictions is that it has so many disassociations that keep us feeling so far apart from our true source, or real self that is connected to the infinite creator. When we perpetuate to keep fear resistant ideas to addiction in this way we are creating a worse disharmony in our body self simultaneously. So labeling to define addictions as not a good thing is giving it the beliefs of fear that keeps us fighting it, triggers guilt feelings and all kinds of limited energy of judgments. We then are fighting against addictions which is totally out of harmony of our natural infinite self of an orgasmic state.

In the light of the wisdom to know that nothing really matters except for the thoughts we choose. Whether we are aware or unaware of what we are giving meaning to begin with of any idea, let alone just addictions.

It is almost like a backward climb that uses fear and limits to get us to the same heavenly state that really is our physical purpose on these journeys in physical.

Don't let me loose you here if your beliefs are screaming no way, instead just keep an open mind if this information is not making sense for you yet. Think of your old beliefs as unclear fog you still have some value in and as you open up to this information it may be a little foggy at the start when trying to see through the fog. When it becomes to resonate with you will see it more clearly just as you do when in fog and it dissipate.

So some things that are label as addictions are alcohol, cigarettes, illegal drugs, sex, but now we have medications that seem to be more lethal and dangerous then the illegal ones. We have all heard the commercials of their warning of symptoms. What is that? It sounds ridiculous because taking a pill that has worse side affects than the reason or illness to take the medication in the first place. Who are they trying to fool?

The legal drugs are so blended into accepted reality under the illusion of being for our best interest for healing when so much evidence comes back in proving it causes more deaths per year instead. So we will leave that for now because whole books are written on it.

Though I would like to mention that when another person goes on to dictate to me that I should being seeing a doctor for yearly physical check ups. Or I should take medication for whatever disharmony is going on in my body. Apparently that's okay, that's the way it is and how I should be doing it. Yet I have not been to a doctor for almost 20 years and have not taken any pills or medication of any kind for that amount of time. Should I go back to believing what others give meaning to associate with everything?

No, because I have free will just as everyone does to choose the meaning to associate what I desire to give to everything.

Others that are trying to dictate to me of their beliefs of the negative reasons I should be living my life are from their own meanings they've attached to define their meaning of beliefs from others suggestions that conditioned them. But what really amazes me is that they are also on many medicated drugs that they believe is okay but living more sovereign is not. This is only fear based beliefs that most have been conditioned to believe.. I also realize that this is their own reflection and journey because their infinite self knows that nothing matters but the meaning we give it. I also realize it is always in very loving a good intentions of their beliefs, they only want to help.

I also realize that if I attract that kind of dictating then it is up to me to notice and clear up my vibration, my energy that attracted that experience to me. So it is always an opportunity in every experience but also to know that through our own wisdom we are not altering our bliss, only expanding it.

In the media it seems that the individuals who are caught in the addiction behavior seem to get more attention then good behavior. Only because our planet still has invested more value in beliefs of fear and judgments. Which results in defenses which in a loving unconditional world would be quite the opposite that it is now. Yet most are still in the state of being in the trap of the paradox of judging good or bad, right or wrong instead of just acceptance and love.

Sex Addicts

Let us now get back to other addictions labeled as sex addicts, individuals who have more then one partner whether sexually or just as intimate friends. We'd really have to leap decades ahead to view how, why and what is going on now to see that it all does have a higher evolutionary purpose for these types of defined addictions. As they are the breaking ground, so to speak in evolution because in infinite consciousness there is never any ownership or jealousy or committing to owning any other then our own self. That is just another conditioned belief that has sustained humanity for so long.

More Addictions

More addictions as washing one's hands all of the time or watching too much television. We know the list is so literally endless, if we do something that another does not agree with or is conditioned to believe as wrong, it is labeled as an addiction.

It was only 40 to 50 years ago that smoking was cool, everyone done it, it was a pleasure thing not an addiction. Then it became to be of no more pleasure and reversed to become to the point it is now, disgraceful to be caught smoking. This is another creating an association to give it meaning to define it to be cool or then disgusting. Really in it's true nature like everything, its just neutral and has no meaning until we give it meaning. Or what about wine it has changed in conditioned beliefs to now be good for us because research has proven it to be.

Victim of Conditioning Suggestions

So who has conditioned the population to follow along with those beliefs that has become the rules and conditions to dictate all these false beliefs to us? Why do they do it? Because we allow them to because we are not our own authorities, we have become the victim of suggestions.

If research says it is good for us, everyone does it, if research then turns it around and says it is bad for us, many follow with that idea, no matter what they intuitively feel is true. This is referred to as conditioning. Whatever is dictated as truth many agree then it must be and it becomes what many seem to follow!

So we became a society that is so far removed from our true real source of God or Creator then we realize. And the THEY, who are in all forms of our government, health systems, monetary systems, we are not able to just pick a few, it is trickled throughout all of our systems.

Taking Your Power Back

So it is not important to know who THEY are, it is important to realize what is being suggested as conditioning and then take your own responsibility if you want to believe it or not. So whoever THEY may be can be perceived as a great opportunity for us to take our power back and feel actually grateful. Yes grateful that whoever is doing the conditioning is giving us the opportunity to know we have a choice to believe or not believe. To take it to an orgasmic state of nothingness and instead make it blissful, the most beneficial state to be in.

The Benefits of Knowing We Are Creators Creating Our Reality

If people do not know how reality is created then they will be easily enslaved and be followers believing everything that authority tells them. We can have our own wisdom and authority for our own selves if we become wise to it. Instead of letting them label the idea that addictions are bad and will kill you if you do not do something about it. And anyone teaching that addictions will never lead us to heaven or god is another bogus one. Even though I am sure that the ones who are teaching it are teaching it under what they believe is loving intentions, however it is still ego altered judgment teachings of fear attachments. Is it worth becoming sick from or even dying as a result of conditioned beliefs? Maybe if it's in your infinite blueprint plan? If the addiction is creating more fear and resistance then its going in the opposite direction of love and orgasmic living.

Ask yourself, where does free will come into any of these fear limited beliefs about Addiction?

Nowhere, it just does not!

Where is the state of orgasmic bliss of eternal love in all of these fear beliefs in addiction?

It is the opposite, teaching to fear what others tell you to fear, to conform to what they want you to conform to. Then we can also realize that since everyone has their own journey, we can take our power back by using all of this as an opportunity to know our own self.

Okay, so let's get back to the idea of addictions and addictions being bad and will never take you to a natural heavenly blissful feelings. Let us take a look at this from a different expanded sovereign free will point of view of how an adult mature evolved creator would be doing with all this.

Have you read the article from Shirley McClain's web site of a women who decided to quite smoking at 117 years old? She lived in the 1940's when smoking was pleasurable and cool, then she was still around when it became twisted in reverse and dictated that smoking is no longer pleasurable and cool, it is disgusting and bad for our health. So she lived through the variety of the conditioning dictated suggestions, however never fell into the dictating beliefs. She just lived from her own real self and what she defined as pleasure for her, regardless what others were suggesting.

She believed in herself not what anyone else dictated to her, she is a role model of not allowing others to give meaning to anything, but to give one's own meaning to everything in the way that feels most empowering for our own self. She quit smoking at 117 years old when she wanted and decided for her own reasons not because conditioning dictated her to quit decades earlier.

So addictions did not concern her, instead she is living her life to the fullest of what she creates to believe and enjoys as her pleasures instead. This is the reason that I find labeling things we find pleasure in as addictions can alter our bliss, our natural daily orgasmic feelings. Why would anyone want to do that? Because they just do not know how powerful they really are.

What then really does addictions have to do with pleasure, heaven and orgasm?

Only the meaning we give to describe what it will do, that is it. That is how powerful we are. So powerful yet without realizing that when we allow others to dictate how we should define and give meaning to anything when instead of choosing for one's own self and instead letting others choose for us. We must realize when we do that we are giving our god creating given ability away. If there was a real true reality to sin, which I don't believe there is, it would be not knowing and being your own authority and creator of your own reality. And even not knowing that wisdom will always be forgiven from an infinite creator.

Perceiving More as A Good Thing

When we have experienced it enough to know this is the way it is then it is easy to let go of the fear based energy that dictates the ideas of addictions. So more and more is a good thing if we become in the heavenly orgasmic state of being instead of being in the negative or weak fear state of being.

I ask you one more question to ponder, can you experience orgasm if you are a "so called" addict?

Really think about it now from a sovereign attitude of thought. If we can experience heaven, bliss, the ecstasy of orgasm no matter what type of 'so called' person we are, then what is that also trying to tell us, what message is that trying to get to us?

If anyone even Hitler can experience orgasm then what is the underlying message here?

It would seem to be totally removed with no judgments or conditions at all. And how do we perpetuate ourselves not to keep falling into the pit of conformity and rise once and for all above it? You will find out more in the next chapter.

CHAPTER 5

OUR FUTURE NOW LIVING FROM INFINITY

We all know of a paradise that so many desire to live life in bliss, feeling so heavenly, being lifted from the drudgery day of have to do and must do's. Whether it is from our jobs or unfulfilled life we are living, relationships that have gone sour yet many continue to be enslaved in. Whatever the drudgery may be for everyone can be unique or common, it will always be what we define it to be.

Most individuals do believe they must escape to a paradise of physical destinations as going to the tropical islands if they live in the cold climate of environments. There are a few who define paradise of escaping to the cold environments to bask in the snow. So paradise is unique for individuals depending on what they refer their meanings that define for them to be fun and paradise.

For writers it can be the majestic spell bound state while writing with a infinite flow of exuberant messages coming from within into words on pages as I am experiencing in my paradise of doing right now. For musicians it can be playing an instrument the escape in the flow of the experience of rhythms and notes inwardly flowing outwardly so natural through their fingers through the instrument and hearing the sounds created.

It can be in our first coffee in the morning. As we are smelling it as it is brewing and the sensuous experience of being divinely one as we are sipping it's flavor of it on our lips and into our mouths. With the flow of appreciation as the taste buds orgasmic basking in the sensations and we feel the experience in it's orgasmic divinity. Whatever or whenever we experience things or situations that way it allows us the experience of blissful, heavenly, infinite feelings of experience. These feelings, this state of being we are in when we experience bliss through all things other then sexual orgasm of bliss is all one of the same, just derived from different experiences. It is the same feeling, the same state we feel into our daily lives.

Orgasm as the Hidden Key to Paradise of Bliss

We must come to realize once and for all that orgasm is the seeming hidden key to unlocking the way to allowing that ecstatic state of feeling into experiencing it in everything we do. It is there for that reason, not just for a moment, but as a reminder from our infinite source. It is the highest vibration, the highest state one can experience to be in, yet most reserve it only for sexual experience.

It is once we ponder the notion, the information that transforms to wisdom that it will start to make sense, that to feel that good for a few moments is meant for something more. That expansion of more is to realize and bring these feelings into our daily lives. Live the orgasmic experience with everything we do. Once you realize and experience it enough times you just know and resonate with it too, it has always been there for us to know and to do, I call it orgasmic living

Transforming mundane chores into orgasmic experiences

Let us take a mundane experience of putting the trash out for collection, for many it is a dreary job that has to be done each week. We can choose new ways of doing it compared to the normal way and that makes all the difference in the experience of what we get out of it. We can take the trash out in the dreary rational old way of habit or create a new habit by doing it in the most sensual orgasmic heavenly way to be experienced.

If we sing or hum a song while collecting the trash and think thoughts similar to the appreciation of the person who picks it up and how grateful we can feel for their services. It is because of the service offered that allows us to keep trash limited from filling our area that we live.

If we become creative which is opening up to allow creative thoughts to come through as inspiration, we can find many inspirational thoughts like this to use. Such an old way of drudgery has within it the divine golden key that orgasmic opportunity can shine a light on for a new creative ways to do anything in our lives.

Taking out the trash then becomes more of a pleasure and if you really take it to the max of creativity you could even experience an orgasmic feeling of bliss. To really bring it into a high loving vibration you can go through the motion starting with self love by lovingly taking out the garbage.

Oh I know this may sound a bit outrageous, however if we think about how we can experience orgasmic feeling just by choosing better thoughts, we then know it makes all the difference in our experiences. And these better thoughts instead of the old ones will bring out the same love feelings that orgasm give us. That way we are being sensual with our rhythm act of an art how we choose to put out the garbage, it takes on a high love vibration.

So just by thinking about the sexual act or orgasms state of being feelings without even having sex, just thinking about having it can bring on the feeling for many, so what is the difference with using it the same way for everything. It creates all drudgery chores to a higher level and a pleasurable enjoyment.

Orgasmic Ways of Putting out the Trash

Let us revise and observe it by doing it in a creative inspired loving way. As we pick up the bag we notice our hands and how sensual they are as they pick up the bag or container. Then watch our legs move so flexible along and how lovingly they move without our commands, they are just there always supporting our body. As you hum a favorite song you hear the sound of your hum from you magnificent voice, whether you're a good singer or not is not the point, and then that depends on the meaning you give it, remember. So you appreciate that you can hum and sing and have memory to do it from. If you choose to go even further and put out the trash while the sun is rising, you can become one with the beautiful magnificent experience of the prism array of colors that are illuminating in the sky. You can experience the dark turning into day so in flow. You can observe the happy chirping of birds awakening and also being one with the new morning.

When you really get into the mood, into the feel of it all, in this kind of a blissful orgasmic present state you can even feel your body responding if you take notice. You are feeling lightly lifted, happier just to be alive and to be able to experience all these natural things that are going on. And your body is also a part of it all when we consciously are aware of it's natural movement. Feel the blissful orgasmic electrical magnetism with sensations moving through your body, be aware and notice it. Feel the way your clothes feel against your skin can be almost like foreplay to triggering us to the momentum of the orgasmic blissful sensations just by being aware.

You're probably close to orgasm now, just keep going with the flow and allow it to release into that ecstatic feeling to implode without the physical release into everything you are doing. And keep the expansion of it going.

If you did this every week and every time you took out the trash what would eventually happen is for starters it would become habitual, you would also associate taking out the trash and any trash to be a sensual orgasmic experience. Taking out the trash would become so pleasurable that you'd desire to put it out daily. It would becomes so associative and memorable from the intense emotional feelings that recorded the memory of it in your soul. You may find that when you watch a commercial about trash it would trigger that arousal of feelings of bliss.

Imagine a co-worker or friend talking about trash and you get a huge sensual smile on your face and your friend would wonder what the heck was going on with you. Little do they know that just the mention of trash makes you smile and feel so blissful and brings on the flow of heavenly feelings.

Orgasmic Bliss for Everything

Now this is just one thing, taking out the trash. Now imagine all of the things you can do this with, brushing your teeth and really being intimate and one with the tooth brush as it gently messages your beautiful gums and teeth.

Taking notice of all the moments in your life in everything you do that you can transform all of it into these orgasmic experiences. This is bringing the heavenly feeling of orgasm into our daily life. The key was always there for us to use and we just we're too busy surviving and thinking limited non creative fear motivated thoughts through our processes instead.

Think about how much more you would be smiling throughout the day. As a result you may also notice that many of your little irritations will not be so irritating. You will also notice that little body pains you would feel on a daily basis just seem to have disappeared because feeling this good most of the time is the greatest of natural medicine for the body. All the trillions of body cells are so flowingly moving and responding also to all these feelings too. So the cells are no longer fighting for anything as in stress instead they become a orgasmic dance of healthy and vibrancy as a result. It is not only just a most magnificent feeling when the body takes on that magnificent glow of bliss too?

The first few times you try this your rational old mind filled with old beliefs may try to talk you out of it, but it likes to feel down and depressed about all the drudgery, its just an emotional habit played out too long. We have to lift ourselves up by going past those thoughts. Love and accept those old thoughts and let them go, then insert the new infinite conscious thoughts that are streaming from orgasmic realities. Then each time we are feeling better and better, those thoughts melt away easily till one day they are completely gone.

If you even become concerned about what this may do to your sex life as you may have ponder the notion that if your start to feel this in everything you do through your day then will you still want sex in the normal way? In my experience I have found it is even heightened to more orgasmic levels, almost beyond multiple. It becomes better then ever and you will also experience it once you bring orgasm into your daily life too.

Transforming Stress to Orgasmic Bliss

Imagine all the stress that is transformed into bliss. Someone starts yelling at you and saying things you disagree with, you just smile at them as you automatically take notice how occupied they are in their anger. Yes even someone's anger is no longer taken personally because you can transform that perception of anger into an orgasmic experience. How? By using it an opportunity to do just that transform it in you powerful present moment to something blissful which can be using empathy, now isn't that a more intimate orgasmic perception. You become to perceive it as they are so intimate with their anger and that event takes on a different spin. A spin that triggers a smile on your face. The other person will either just walk away or question you about the way you are responding, which you know is the orgasmic blissful response. Either way it is a winning situation of experience, orgasmic responses always are.

Whether you choose to just read these sentences or do the actual rethinking to bring your life to orgasmic bliss is totally free will and up to each individual. I know that just from reading this it is stimulating feelings that can not be denied, I know you will ponder it and even a bit of pondering changes things a bit at a time.

Until there comes a time when you walk by a mirror and really see the infinite creator in yourself and you smile and just blurt out to the mirror, wow I sure do love you. Not just a fleeting moment, but it will be genuinely heart felt and that sparkling self love will flow outward not only in everything you do but also in everyone one you encounter.

This is living a orgasmic life, everyday in everyway, unlocking the key finally to the heavenly bliss of orgasm, what I know it was really intended for us in the first place.

Living from Infinity

Tools are objects we use to build something to get us more easily to the end result of what we desire to build. Tools are not the power in and of themselves they are only neutral like anything else. Just as an object or vehicle or medium is, the power we put into the tools we use to get us to where we desire to go or the end result of what we are building So we can perceive our physical body to be similar as a tool. Our body embodies a small part of our massive infinite self in this journey of physical reality for our physical experiences.

Eventually we will also desire to let go of the tools and we will just BE our Real Natural Infinite Selves.

Let's use the analogy of building a house, we use the blueprints, tools, and machinery that we need to get there, once the house is built we no longer need the tools, unless for repairs. Just as the tools for building while we are evolving to an orgasmic life, there may be times when we fall a little backwards, that is okay as we continue to evolve to knowing everything is neutral. We may pick up some tools again maybe for old times sake or when the need arise to repair us, so to speak from limiting judgment of beliefs. Just as we use tools to build a house it can be similar to the tools we use as beliefs, limiting memories from our subconscious programming, they are like worn out tools that we may not need to use any longer. The only importance is the wisdom to know that they are only tools and it is our own being that really matters when it comes to creating and living an orgasmic life.

Many tools that have been handed down through the ages of humanity and presently been re-taught can fall into the headings of psychic abilities. Tools such as meditation, visualization, attitude, intention, focus, attention, law of attraction, energy, synchronicity, spoon bending, fire walking and quantum physics, orgasm and so on. There is an enormous quantity of tools, too many to mention but the ones you choose to work with are just tools and whatever you choose to work with that works best for yourself. All that the tools do is help us learn and practice to become one with what we desire for our experiences to experience.

When we are practicing our abilities on perfecting that we create our reality and become of the wisdom that we are deliberately creating and observing our creations then any or all the tools will get us there. It is only a matter of getting our attention so focused one hundred percent zoomed in that we arrive at the same gap, zone of the infinite state where time and space collapse into infinity, the zone of orgasm.

All the tools will bring us to that state when we become perfected through practice, just like all practicing does is gets us better and better at something. You will eventually get to the point where you could say a word and the word brings you are into that state. We can choose to stay in that orgasmic feeling state of being.

Is it any wonder that orgasm and organic are so closely related in their spellings and definition. Also keep in mind that meanings are only tools too as a way to show us signs that we are on the right track of our Infinite Source or that we might be going in the opposite direction.

You become the empowered being when you are in your Natural Infinite Self state of being in physical embodiment for the great experience of it. Just what I think orgasm was designed to do for us originally, which was for us to remember that this was our original purpose of inspiration. Even though our original purpose we may have begun with was to remind ourselves to remember when we are disillusioned in our physical bodies from our original infinite source or self. To recall the infinite memory that orgasm would trigger the remembrance because it is so heavenly of a state to be in of it's experience.

All the tools can bring you to that state like a magnet because when we use any of the tools that is what they do, they are like a magnet that will pull us in by keeping us focused on one thing. When we are in that state we can easily come out of it too, just as a magnet can attract it can also repel and push us out of that gap, or state.

The Tool of Meditation

Let us take a look a meditation, it is also a tool, we get our self to focus into a no zone of no time, no space, no feeling. Just as orgasm is also a tool to get us to that same state, the only difference is that orgasm is a more excited tool to get us there and many only stay in that state of a few moments.

Meditation is a tool that takes us into that state of being with no excitement, it's a silencing type of tool, remember all tools can get us to the same state, these are just two different tools. Meditation is one tool and orgasm is another.

Just as physical tools, we could use a manual screw driver or a electric screw driver, both do the same thing, its just that one is easy to use then the other. Even though different tools do different jobs as you could use a hammer to screw a screw into wood but the result will be sloppier. Just as meditation will be a better tool for some and yet for others orgasm may be a better tool to get to that gap, into Source or the ecstasy of heavenly bliss.

How about thought being as a tool? To me thought would also seem like a tool to use to get us into the gap of heaven. Because thoughts are going on all the time, they are recycled and since it is approximated that we can have over 70,000 a day, depending on what we are doing.

Buddha monks may have extremely less thoughts because they spend most of their time during their days in the gap, which they refer to as a meditative state. However as we now know or are learning that the meditative state is being in the gap but meditation is the tool to get to the gap. The important thing here is that if thoughts are also tools then we can choose what thoughts we choose to focus on. When we focus on thoughts that we desire to manifest then we choose to think only in alignment with our desire as if it is already manifested.

Spoon Bending

Let us add in spoon bending whether using you hands to bend when it gets soft or if we just use our energy focused through intention without touching it to physically bend it as in telekinesis. The spoon is a tool, our intention is also a tool, our connection to our power is the connection to Source which is the orgasmic state, or heavenly state we keep ourselves in when we do the bending.

Now we can sit and look at that spoon for hours and nothing will happen, once we get into that gap of Source that is where the power is, in a moment is when the bending occurs. In a moment! It's immediate! It takes letting go of all tools to get into that infinity orgasmic gap. And it is all individually unique depending on our beliefs which dictate our own level of what we accept of how long it will take or if we even do it. For children they can do it quick and easily, they have less attachments to rational ego thoughts, which means they have less memories stored of doubts. Children may still have quicker access to the Infinite Source memories then adults that have stored so many conditioned memories that have created beliefs.

For others who's left brain is more dominant it may take allot longer to convince the rational mind that it is possible, for some they may never do it, yet everyone has the capability to do it.

Synchronicity

Another tool as synchronicity can show us signs that we are on our path to something greater. Things seem to align and synch into whatever we are doing. I used to keep a journal of synchronicities until too many a day were occurring to keep track of. That is what starts to happen, signs show up everywhere in everything we do when we get into that alignment with Source. Again it is another tool to show us like sign posts if we are in alignment with the infinite gap or not in alignment. We just seem to rise up to such an orgasmic state of bliss and appreciation that all go hand in hand, all come from the heart and expand into everything. When we get that aligned it just comes so naturally. It is no wonder that **come** is such a powerful inviting word and when spelt differently as cum, we start to see the synchronicity of orgasmic living.

Different Meanings for Everyone

In many religions we will find different flavored varieties of beliefs concerning everything including what may be referred to as heaven. That is the reason I refer to heaven as bliss because it strips away many attached dogma that religions have attached in defining heaven compared to bliss. Bliss is more neutral in that sense and released of attachments except for the high vibrational feelings that flowingly go with it. This is what some religious dogma contains, judgments with superstition, however I am quite sure that many who are reading this book already have passed and broken down many of those dogmatic beliefs. If not then you may be on your way. Though it may also take some time and awareness to break free in allowing old ritual habits of beliefs to collapse for the new potential ones to be replaced. You may even find the old beliefs have comfort zones that also become released for you to be more comfortable as your beliefs about orgasm evolves.

If you are resonating with this concept, this wisdom, then you surely have expanded your consciousness to know more of the truths that have been awaiting to know.

We can easily see that beliefs are so expanded and everyone does have different beliefs in regards to everything, especially if there is no religious factoring in the mix. Then individuals are even freer in their natural flexibility and have expanded their beliefs in many different directions which allows orgasm to lead the way.

Infinite Source

So I think by now you are getting a leading edge here on all the variety of tools and how all or any of the tools that are available that we choose to use are not where the power is. The power is in the Infinite Source and even though we are starting to feel and experience that power in a more conscious aware state. I am sure it still boggles most of us still to get a comprehensive grip in trying to realize how powerful that Infinite Source is.

The experiences we are having with Infinite Source is so amazing, seeming out of this world, which orgasm really is. It is being out of the ego world of conditions of subconscious memories and just experiencing the ecstasy of heaven.

Let me express it from my heart with another new word, it is so **zamactrifying**. Yes that feels better to try to define it with a heart felt expression and more creatively, it is so zamactrifying of a feeling to be in that we desire more and more of it. And I would imagine we can because what else is infinity through orgasm all about?

So no matter what tools we choose to use, they will get us there and it is also our choice how long we desire to stay there. It may be for only moments or extending it into our daily lives into as much as we can. You are the chooser, the chosen one to decide for you own self whatever you choose to do, and that sure is empowering no matter what. Just because the orgasmic capability is there for us whenever we choose to use it.

So pack up your tools, or bring no tools and let's go on the next wild ride into the next chapter.

CHAPTER SIX

\ \ \ \ \ \ \ \ \ \ \ \ \ \ \ \ \ \ \ \

HEART AND BODY'S BENEFITS OF ORGASMIC BLISS

Your heart is be the best indicator for making the best decisions by following your heart, it also extends life. When we are in orgasmic bliss all of our body cells stay in harmony which creates sustained health and longevity. When we alter from our blissful state our body is creating the opposite in our body, a disharmonious state. The difference literally becomes life or death.

Body's DNA is Being Reprogrammed Depending on our Responses that Becomes our State of Being

All disease is a result of altering from our bliss and if we do not transform those fearful thoughts and feelings, disease worsens and creates premature death. It is now known that our body's DNA holds information that our body cells respond to is not predetermined as believed in the past. Our DNA is so flexible and is dependant on how we respond to everything that occurs in our lives that literally changes the information in our DNA. Bruce

Lipton has shared this information publicly and it is so worth further learning if you have not yet studied the knowledge. Your body's DNA is changing as a result to your daily thoughts, reactions and how you feel. This is so empowering and is the greatest benefit to being aware and keeping yourself in an orgasmic blissful state of being.

Heart Awareness

Your heart is always showing you feedback by how you feel. All it takes is being aware throughout the day to get yourself back on track.

Stop right now and think of a time when you felt the most joy, excitement and love. Linger in the thoughts long enough until it generates the emotions into feeling it within your heart. Do you feel the heart expanding and feeling light with love?

Now do the opposite think of something that scares you presently, something that when you think about it stirs up emotions that make you feel so tense.

You literally can feel the difference and though this is just a simple exercise, it is so empowering profound. How many times are you really self aware like this throughout your day? Simple experiences like this that are so profound usually go unnoticed, especially not being aware of how you are reacting to others and situations. Yet it creates all the difference in how your body is harmonizing or disharmonizing that is creating your body to be stressed or in bliss. By taking notice you then realize and feel the differences immensely.

This is the reason we have feelings, that we are feeling beings, it not only gives us the feedback for ourselves it also generates and programs as information into our DNA from our heart first. It is our heart that generates emotions that are running freely around in our body and it is the heart that gathers the emotions and creates them into feelings we then feel.

Whenever you want to know anything, instead of thinking from your head, think to feel from your heart and you will always get the best potential answer to follow. That is the reason for the sayings, "Follow your Heart" "Follow your Bliss" knowing the hidden key that unlocks the door for orgasm to create bliss that generates through our hearts and affects our DNA's information that is constantly being programmed that expands throughout the rest of the body.

Heart Bliss Tuner

Dan Winter has invented a heart bliss tuner that actually measures the body's response to bliss, compassion and love. His work intensively shows how responding blissfully literally affects the heart that then affects the DNA and the rest of the body. And also how it extends life and creates evolving by activating what was in the past referred to as junk DNA. That supposed junk DNA is actually not junk but what we could refer to as DNA that has been turned off that we can activate to turn on. This creates our capability to experience what has been referred to as extraordinary abilities of psychic phenomenon.

Feel from Your Heart

So start or continue to think from your heart by noticing how you feel when pondering in decisions about anything. For anything you want an answer, just ask the question and allow your heart to answer you by how it feels, resonates to you. This does take being self aware and you will find through repetition that eventually you would not do anything without checking with your heart first. It will become just as natural as when you were not aware, to become aware, all it takes is some practice. And this practicing can also expand your life span, the choice and free will is always up to you.

CHAPTER 7

REVERSE AGING THROUGH ORGASM

Let us really take a inside look at our bodies and the aging process. Our bodies are made up of trillions of cells, biology and science approximates over 70 trillions cells is what our bodies are made up of. So really think about this for more than a fleeting moment, our bodies, yours that is here right now reading this contains over 70 trillion living cells that keeps your body functioning while we are busy doing other things.

Even when we are not aware of what our trillions of body cells are doing all the time, it is just by realizing how miraculous it works on how it sustains us minutely is amazing. That in itself is the most incredible thing that is occurring every second that we are in our physical bodies. Just pondering in this exuberant magnificence is worth pondering how all these separate cells are either in harmony of functioning as in healthy cells of a body or out of harmony cells as in a dis-eased body.

When we ponder the wonderings ... where do all these body cells get their commands, their instructions to perform in how they create our body? This may be the most important question you may ever ask yourself because the answer is where the power really is.

The commands, the instructions is from our self.

Then you may wonder what self? The thinking self, the one that is choosing what thoughts that are giving the commands, whether done automatically or through consistent awareness?

Let us realize that our brain is only a receiver of information. If we are to compare it to a radio, then the receiver is not the whole radio object, the receiver is one part of it's unit. It allows the radio, which is the total object that holds the receiver unit within that then allows the transmitting to take place. By the push of a button we then can change a channel instantly to be able to listen to a channel of music we enjoy. Our brain in our body is the same, it sits at the top of our body in our head processing infinite bits of data of information 24/7. Constantly processing and transmitting data of information through our nervous system. Which is also connected and transmits to all trillions of living cells and organs continuously and consistently instantaneously.

Just as a radio uses the receiver unit to pick up different frequencies of channels from a massive variety of channels, is the same as our brain as the receiver picking up different frequencies of thoughts as the channels to choose from. Except these channels are of thoughts, and it is approximated that we are choosing about 70, 000 thoughts a day, so that would be 70.000 thoughts we choose to pick the channels we are tuning into. The bandwidth being of all consciousness that's infinite to choose from, yet if we choose negative channels, negative thoughts then we get negative feelings as a result. Just as if you choose a certain frequency of let's say

94.7fm then you will get jazz, however if you choose 94.7 on the am bandwidth you may get static or whatever is on that channel.

So if we desire the channel of thoughts that would pick up the informational data for either not aging or reversing the aging process that we have to pick those channels of thoughts from the massive infinite thoughts in consciousness. Then focus on those thoughts which would be similar to changing and picking a channel on a radio. Once we pick that channel of thoughts it will give us the information to do what we desire to do, give us the data, the information that pertains to that desire. The information is that the body is a fluid constant changing vessel for creating what we desire to have it become and or sustain it to be.

The brain is not the part that does the creating of the changes. The brain only gives the commands from what we think about most of the time that becomes our belief systems, the message to the central nervous system that then gives the messages to the cells. It is like a chain reaction taking place constantly.

Using the Power in the Present Moment of Now

If we want to be more consciously aware of the thoughts we are choosing then its best not to be so concerned about where all those old programs came from previously that we believed in for so long. Instead it is easier and more powerful to work from this point onward which means using the power of the present moment to expand on.

Just as when you turn to a radio channel you desire to hear, you do not care or think about what the channel was called 70 years ago, you just enjoy what is being transmitted now for you to enjoy. The same is with old beliefs and thoughts, it does not matter where they came from because the infinite memory bank of consciousness of all humanity and more dimensional memories forever to choose from. And that's an infinite variety.

The most important part is knowing it is in the NOW that you can choose to enjoy the channel you have chosen. The same for our bodies. We can choose any thoughts we desire if it is something we enjoy and have fun with, get excited about, feel in bliss about, feel that orgasmic feeling about. It does not matter where it comes from, it is only up to ourselves to pick that uplifting channel of thoughts and go with it and keep the orgasmic feelings going. It is in that channel that will create the brain to receive and transmit the message to the nervous system and all the cells in the body. If we sustain that momentum, that channel, those frequencies of thoughts will be what the body cells will work in the response from and that is how the body cells will be, young. This is how we know it is not impossible or outrageous to know that we can reverse our aging process and sustain our body to maintain that output of energy of youthfulness when we choose that orgasmic feeling to be in.

All of the body cells, trillions of them, I love the reference that Bruce Lipton gives that our body is like a city and our cells are like the individuals who make up the city, it is a community. If we view it in that way then we can easily recognize that whatever we give our attention of thoughts to we are affecting our bodies by giving those commands for it to perform. While simultaneously creating the energy flow in how we attract everything else to us along our days and circumstances and situations.

So it is not only about reversing the aging process. Reversing the aging process is a part of everything else that is going on and from what state of being we are in to begin with that also effects everything else in our lives. We cannot just desire not age or reverse the aging process if we keep supporting the old beliefs we have in aging that gives the commands that the body is suppose to deteriorate. In other words if you look at yourself in the mirror and think oh my face is getting older looking, that's an automatic reaction from old beliefs. We need to look in the mirror in the perception that our face is already looking younger, trusting and knowing it does have that ability when we recreate new beliefs to not only support reverse aging but also choose the new thoughts that will sustain it. And being in the orgasmic state can do just that when we realize the orgasmic state is being in an infinite state of no time in space.

The hidden key we will find is to live from an orgasmic state of being from the thoughts into feelings when we awake. Then to continue the same way throughout the rest of the day. Then we will realize that whenever we alter from the orgasmic state we become disharmonious for everything, not just aging. What we choose to think about everything will makes all the difference from our bodies point of view, from the cells that are connected to all other cells and nervous system that is connected to our brain.

Sustaining orgasmic feelings of bliss, ecstasy, heavenliness, means instead of reacting to limiting negative thoughts of beliefs, and instead respond to everything as an opportunity. Like an invitation to return to the orgasmic feeling all of the time is what will create the body to no longer age. In a sense you are taking heavenly orgasm with you along in everything in your daily life through the channel of thoughts you have consciously chosen. Orgasm was created to do just that for us, that is the hidden key that can lead us into no longer the temptation to alter ourselves from that blissful state of being. To sustain it because it is easy to when you realize how good it feels and all the benefits it has from staying in it. It will become more and more natural the more that you sustain and bask in it.

In this simplistic example, someone drives by you and cuts you off in traffic and yells and gives you the finger, what do you do? The old way is to react from old habitual behavior of getting angry and then telling the story about it all day, how mean and angry that person was, how rude. That keeps the energy going, the telling the story keeps the energy of being altered from an orgasmic state.

The best way in dealing with that situation would not have it happened at all because we'd know that nothing can just happens to us. We know that everything is vibration attracting us to what we get from what we put out. And of course if it does happen to us, by being aware we will take notice, just as we would a static signal on our radio. Would we continue to listen to the static noise? No you'd change the channel. This is the same as changing our channel by switching to the orgasmic channel of bliss instead of automatic anger or frustration reactions. When we respond to get our self back to the orgasmic feeling of bliss our body cells are also reacting differently too. It is important not to judge yourself either or the other person, instead use it as a signal or sign that you altered yourself from the blissful state. Then refocus into the desired orgasmic channel again and continue to respond more in the orgasmic way than the automatic ways. This is always a benefit for reversing and sustaining aging because it keeps you from being stressed out. We know that being stressed creates havoc with our body cells which trigger in creating the chemical proteins that creates the aging affect.

So next time a similar situation occurs you get to respond with a big smile to the rude driver. Why? You will smile because the other driver was a blessing to remind you that for a few moments you changed the channel of thoughts. Even though it was only a few moments, it is a very powerful moment of revelation, enough for you to realize that the situation took you off track and altered your blissful heavenly state. In that powerful moment you can also use it to get yourself back into that orgasmic state again. But then a few moments later you may be altering your bliss without realizing it, you may have started thinking about a bill unpaid or a chore you have to do. It was that channeling away with choosing different thoughts other then the orgasmic bliss for a little bit that changed the frequency, the channel without you realizing it. So now you smile and be thankful that you noticed the alteration again, reminding you to respond the new way. While simultaneously through this new process, your body cells are staying also in the same orgasmic harmonious blissful state and continue to dance around in bliss. And then what is the result of that? No aging, no stress, still blissful and learning.

When we compare it to reacting the old way that would of taken the cells out of bliss and into a stressed state which then starts the process of dis-ese, which could just be a cold or flu or headache, depending on how long it takes you to get back to that ease of orgasmic state. So we can see that it really is affecting everything in our body and creations consistently.

Minutely you start to notice and realize that Nothing Is Worth Altering Your Orgasmic Bliss for, NOTHING!

You start to notice that you are looking younger, your face is glowing and creases of wrinkles that you noticed a day or two ago are softening. Then you notice a few days later they are almost gone, then a stranger tells you that they thought you were 35 when you are really suppose to be 55. You start to feel lighter and notice that you do weigh lighter on the scale then you did a week ago.

You also notice that pains in your neck and back and other spots of your body are no longer there, you feel good all over. You also notice that you no longer need those magnifying glasses to read close. Your memory has become sharper and more clear and you are smiling more and also noticing that almost everyone you encounter has that same kind of smile and disposition, shine about them. And if for a instant someone rude or negative comes along so easily you can smile at them and know exactly for all the reason because you are a orgasmic being filled with love and it is becoming to overflow, except for some minor signals that may come along again just as reminders.

It is the miraculous magic of heavenly orgasm brought into your daily life, responding from that orgasmic state continuously just because it feels so blissfully good?

CHAPTER 8

ALL POSSIBILITIES IN ORGASM GAPS

Let us ponder a bit into the information that quantum physics has allowed us to notice about reality. We know that physics is the part of science that scientifically shows us what our physical reality is all about through mathematical measurements. We also know that Einstein said that, Quantum physics of entanglement "is spooky action." If it was spooky to Einstein the genius who revolutionized energy then he knew there was something going on. Something that was trying to show us something unknown to be known that was a bit out of our ordinary perception of reality that we were comfortably accustomed to.

Quantum physics pushes us to the leading edge and then pushes over the edge having everyone well except for the ancient masters who already knew of this wisdom.

How can one particle be a wave and then back to be a property of a particle again? And then be in more then two places at a time?

How can a particle be in one state and then in many other states when it transforms into a wave containing all the original data and information? How is it that an observer of an experiment can effect the result of the experiment by observing it?

Quantum physics, quantum mechanics has leverage to bring us the ordinary to the extra ordinary, the paranormal to become normal. The stalemate of finite to infinite, the three dimension to multidimensional, the impossible to become possible. And for what reason? To evolve, to be on a purposeful journey, collapse the old reality that the majority of conditioned humanity has come upon as a doorway to evolve, pushing the envelope to make the changes needed to evolve into.

Knowing how reality is creating or the nature of reality is to take our power back once and for all. To know that we are the creators looking back at ourselves, to know that we are personally creating our own realities and also simultaneously adding to mass reality.

We are affecting our mass reality collectively by what we think and do on a personal level. We are already past the leading edge of the changes that we are evolving into our reality on planet earth. Which is the plane of existence that is to become awakened from the victim mentality into the sovereign mentality of beings.

We are expanding many things that seemed so impossible that are now becoming possible. We are becoming aware of limited past beliefs of paranormal is becoming widely accepted and experienced by more and more of the population. Explosions of channeler's that are sharing data and information from other realities that are showing us how to evolve and the greater capacities that we hold in our physical embodiment. Gradually it is overflowing bit by bit into the main stream for others to ponder and become curious to know more about reality then the just mere survival sustained through humanity.

Quantum physics open the Pandora box to evolve us to a life of being empowered individually and mass collectively to evolve. Showing us what orgasm is really all about and all the possibilities that were only labeled under fictional. Long enough to sustain momentum so that our brains and embodiment could expand that powerful momentum into our daily lives to no longer see it as fictional but to merge the fiction into facts. To know that our thoughts are energy and whatever we choose to think about is what will energize outwardly in physical to experience.

Orgasm can be viewed in a quantum state of being by the action and the state we experience. When we experience sexual orgasm we are in our bodies, yet for a few moments we feel as if we are out of our bodies into a heavenly state or world. We feel like we are in two places at one time, in our physical bodies yet simultaneously experiencing the sensational feeling of orgasm.

Though most do not question if we really are in two places because it feels as if we left one place and are in another until the orgasm is finished then we are back in our body. It seems as if we instantaneously expand into something more then our bodies can even comprehend because the ecstatic feeling really does feel out of this world. Quite similar to out of body experiences when all fear is removed.

Let us compare it to our daily reality of every day situations and experiences.

If thinking, which creates our believing from a limited automatic consciousness which consists of old recycled thoughts that we are picking up, then our life is going to be experienced as humdrum and routine. We will be picking up thoughts that trigger the old automatic habit of feeling. Feelings like worried, hurried, stressed, pessimistic, depressed, to use the most combined label for it all, we will think, believe and feel as if we are victims. Then we will only notice and receive bits of heaven, bliss, ecstasy when we have sex and that sex reaches to orgasm.

Though there also may be specks of orgasmic feelings when drinking your first coffee which may start to come through but then while one is drinking their coffee they may be sitting there staring at a pile of unpaid behind bills.

What did you just do?

Without realizing it you just said no to continuing with the starting of an orgasmic feeling. When instead you could of stayed longer to bask in the orgasmic feeling. Instead without realizing it you are going to bask in the worry or stress and ruin the state of orgasmic state of being. These are two different states of being.

Now for comparison, not to be judging it but only to have a frame to reference, to be able to observe the difference. How it can really change our feelings from believing we are a victim to realizing we are the cause of the effect we experience?

Another individual who is more consciously aware and is flowing triggers from bliss will drink their coffee, look at the stack of unpaid bills and push them aside. Oh you may be thinking right now, if I push those bills aside that's being not responsible. Just hang on a little longer and I will explain the reason we will actually be more responsible. Those unpaid bills are a creation from an old reality of beliefs, past old thoughts that were chosen without realizing it. So as we continue with the new orgasmic state of being when looking at the bills, we will bask in that bliss feeling, the orgasmic feeling that is arising and keep it flowing. We will realize that any negative thoughts given to the situation is only going to detour or block the creating flow of energy. In other words if we are to choose victim mentality then we know from past experience that it will create more of it, more unpaid bills to come in and also disease the body with unhealthy results. We also can realize that feeling blissful is not only keeping the body cells functioning in harmony and health, but is simultaneously creating a future in the now. With less unpaid bills because the energy will change by transforming to the new orgasmic state and the new creations will start to appear to better feeling reality being created.

Whatever we focus on expands

So we realize that there are two paths, two different ways to approach something and everything. The path will also unfold differently for either way we choose with conscious awareness or in the case of not choosing in awareness then that would be automatic reactions. This is important because when we choose from conscious awareness, we desire to keep sustaining our orgasmic feeling of bliss. And to continue and from that mindset we also will change the course of our day and the state that our body will be in too.

Our day could flow in more bliss and then creativity will also follow with passion too. We will trust our intuition and things will pop up that we will notice and follow which will take us into the territory of ways to resolve the original challenge. So we are then using the challenge as an opportunity to follow and in that path we are sustaining that orgasmic blissful feeling throughout our day. We are attracting by the vibration of our energy more things that will continue along the day to bring more blissful feelings our way. While simultaneously are body cells are sustaining in that orgasmic blissful state our body is also sustaining it's health. The cells are content in harmony, in ease, in the natural state our body functions in when we keep in that orgasmic blissful state.

Following the other path would then be the extreme opposite, actually in resistance to orgasm and our day would appear to have so many negative things happen to us. Like spilling our coffee, rushing to wherever we were going, someone cutting us off in traffic, our body cells are then in a state of stress, disharmony, in a protection mode. In that type of vibration our cells then become stressed because they are huddling together, like sitting on the edge of needing to fight off some thing. Eventually throughout the day the energy may change because something will trigger us to compliment another or we may be given a gift or another driver smiles at us and let us in, it will be something that brings us back to some kind of good feeling.

The easiest way to recognize what is going on is by how we are feeling and if we continue that disharmonious feelings we are eventually going to have body pain. And the body ages also in that state of continued stress or negativity. The face will show it with many lines of wrinkles from so much frowning and stress all from the cells that have picked up the messages of command from the thinker who continues to attach themselves to those stressful thoughts.

If we use the quantum state of orgasm to be in then we go in many directions at once. We use quantum physics as a role modeling to know that we are the observer that is collapsing the particle into a wave that then expands our body to respond to what we desire to observe it to be. Then not only our body but our reality becomes what we observed it to be by the choice of thoughts we chose to attach to and that observation becomes the collapsed particle state again. From solid particles to waves of energy of fluidity back and forth, it is going on all of the time until eventually it becomes an orgasmic habit to be in.

Most of us may not even notice how it is going on all of the time, we are doing it continuously with the thoughts we think, we are taking a infinite wave of consciousness and collapsing it into particle states. Those particle state are what we physically experience as our physical reality and manifestations. Our reality being created from a infinite wave to finite solid mass particle. When we choose throughout our momentum of minute sparking of thoughts in and out through out our days with awareness of what we are choosing we will see the proof. All depending on what we choose to think about, orgasmic state or automatic old data of memories of beliefs that are tainted and limited.

We can choose the state of orgasm of heaven that is connected to infinite source or the state of hell of survival being in a victim state which is more irresponsible. It really is quite simple when you see it from the state of the observer observing and collapsing the wave back and forth. That we are always the observing doing it, individually we are doing it all day long all by our own self. We may think that someone else is doing it to us if they trigger some anger in us from something they may have said, but in real truth of quantum reality, no one can do anything to us unless we allow them. Which simply means that the other person is only a reflection of our own beliefs, they do what they do and if we recognize what they are doing and observe it as a threat then that is how we see reality for our self and it will be created in the experience.

The other person does not make us angry, we use them to blame because that is what conditioned history has role modeled for us. In the quantum orgasmic state we know that no one can do anything to us, it is our own self because if we are in a state of quantum organic bliss then if another does anything, it does not affect us. If it does we learn more about our own self from the experience and more orgasmic bliss expands.

We may realize that we do not resonate with what others do and just accept and allow knowing we are all on our own purposeful journey's. When we choose to stay in our orgasmic state just because it just feels too heavenly good to alter ourselves from it, then eventually we will desire to continue to respond blissfully. We leave everyone else to their own perceptions, it just does not affect us any longer, we become to own that state of orgasm and just love it and it's benefits too much.

CHAPTER 9

EASY MANIFESTATIONS THROUGH ORGASM

All the secrets are out of what many master teachers have knew and taught throughout humanity's history from the ancient traditions that continue presently. Now it is not just a few teachings surfacing it is overflowing into more and more, expanding us to become aware and experience what was only known to a minority in the past.

Law of Attraction teaches us that what we put out in thought and feeling is a vibration and comes back to us, it is up to our own self to be aware by observing what we are thinking that is creating our feelings. It could be referred to as instant karma.

It is when we not only become to know that we create our own reality but have experimented with the knowledge to bring it into our own wisdom through our own experiences. When we have proven it to our own self over and over and can genuinely say from our hearts resonating that we do create our reality even if we still experience what we do not want, we come to know it is our own self that created it.

We are learning how to manipulate physical matter, growing into aware conscious creators and doing it in the most genuinely loving ways. We may have taken the long road through many tools and processes to get us to where we are presently. Though along the way we learned many more unfolding things that we may not have learned if we did not take certain paths.

We know for our own selves and no one or nothing can alter that knowing wisdom because once you know, you just know, there is no tricks or false illusions to hinder that knowing. We allow others to their own journeys as we know one day, or one life, or some ways it will also be known to the rest when they are ready.

What really amazes me is that **orgasm simply is in plain view if we are taking the momentum to notice that orgasm and creating reality is all intertwined.**

The actual process and being in the experience of orgasm shows us how creating really does work. Most of us who have been on the path of the knowledge that we are all creators creating reality and realities, just know that is what we are all doing.

Though many may not have come to that wisdom yet, they are still creating but just not aware from observing and awareness that they are doing it. I'd like to think that the statement "believe it or not" comes into play because whether we believe it or not that we are creating reality does not matter because the seed, the potential to know is always there.

So really being aware to realize that when we experience orgasm it is the same process and the hidden key of how we create reality into physical and without maybe realizing it we are also creating in multiple realities simultaneously too.

Let us in this present powerful moment of now really focus your thought so that it will trigger you to feel orgasm and what it can show you. Even if it is still hidden for you who have not noticed it yet that orgasm intimately has within it the instructions for creating reality.

We will use orgasm and a desire one may have to show the similarities. For an example I will use a desire of mine that I am presently working on, to have my hair grow in its natural color of light auburn instead of the gray that it has been doing for years. I know it is possible because I know of others who are in their 60's of age and still have their hair growing in their natural color.

It is always easier when another individual or more individuals are already doing something we desire, even if they do not know they are doing it, it is being done. For individuals who don't grow in gray hair as they age and continue to grow in their natural color without any desire, then they most probably chalk it up to DNA of hereditary. But now we know through new biology that DNA is being changed by thoughts, it just that flexible.

The biggest challenges we will find is when there is no one else doing something we desire, when we are the first it can be extremely more challenging. Especially if we have the old beliefs that it will be more challenging or the beliefs that it is natural to grow in gray hair through aging.

So my desire is to grow my hair natural instead of the gray that it is now growing into my scalp. By the way I am not choosing it in a vanity way, I am choosing it as an experiment, research to prove to myself that it can be done. So I take my chosen desire and I visualize it for a few intervals throughout the day and anytime the thought of my hair pops into my mind I automatically use it for an opportunity to see my hair already growing in my natural color, no more growing in of gray hair. What I am doing is ignoring what is presently the gray hair and going right to the already manifested desire as fulfilled. Each time I visualize or feel it to be already as I want it I let it go, in totally trust that it just will become.

I refer to this as orgasmic manifesting because we are going into that ecstasy infinite gap when we imagine or visualize. Letting go is a very important part of manifesting, of creating reality the way we desire it to be, just as we must let go to experience orgasm. It is in the letting go with trust that energizes the quantum field of possibilities of waves to solidify it into particle states for it to become.

Foreplay and orgasm

We use foreplay as a tool to get us to the experience or state of being of orgasm, which of course can also be playful. So we use the tool of foreplay in the same way we use the tool of visualization or imagining as a tool to see and feel our desire already manifested. We know that if during or after foreplay we then need to let go to receive the orgasm, if we do not let go we would stay in foreplay or never have the orgasmic experience at all.

It is in the letting go that allows orgasm to flow and climax, literally. The same way that when we visualize and then let it go in the exuberant ecstatic feeling of releasing the visualization, letting go of the desire already manifested and trust that we then will eventually experience the manifestation in physical. The timing it takes is only dependant on our own self and what we believe is possible. So there can also be many attachments to beliefs that create us to assume that it will take different amounts of time depending on our beliefs.

So we can use orgasm's hidden key as revealing the instructions for creating reality by realizing that orgasm is the key to creating. It shows us how to use the foreplay of visualization to generate the momentum of vibration to bring our energy into a frequency that channels into the manifestation we desire. We become the station as a receiving unit to amplify our desire and if we just allow the release, the channel to stay on that frequency without any static from our doubting rational mind, meaning to hold the trust. And hold it and any time we do release, release it in the letting go of orgasmic pleasure of knowing that it will be manifested to our self in physical. Remind yourself to realize that it is in the releasing with trust that your orgasm is coming is when you then bask in its pleasure, which is letting go into the flow of pleasure, of heaven, of bliss, of ecstasy that orgasm brings.

So when we use the foreplay of visualization with intense feelings as if it already is manifested, those feelings is what is the powerful fuel to bring our vibrations needed to manifest quicker.

In the beginning of using orgasm and creating your desire you can also do it literally. In other words, just as you are close to actual orgasm through making love you can allow your mind to focus on your desire already manifested while you experience your orgasm. What you are doing is inserting your desired thoughts into the orgasm experience. This adds a tremendous feeling energy to your desire and you orgasm which is the fuel to manifesting in physical.

Let go, release in the flow of creation for the pleasure of your desire manifested or for the pleasure of orgasm itself overflowing into everything in your life.

CHAPTER 10

\ \ \ \ \ \ \ \ \ \ \ \ \ \ \ \ \ \ \ \

ROUND AND ROUND IN OLD REALITY

When we are stuck in the old reality that we are functioning from of old ways and from old beliefs we become, we are spinning round and round addicted to old emotions. Which come as a result from old thinking patterns. It takes one month to form a new habit, a new pattern but if we are not aware we can slip and slide back into the old ways too easily.

We can use the feelings of the experience of orgasm to lead us out of what becomes the forbidden path we no longer want to take for many reason. Whatever old pattern we have been choosing thoughts to think with whether it be eating for comfort, always lack of money, or fall into depression when things do not go the way we want.

It is essential to become so fine tuned in awareness of how the old attached thoughts become to create the feelings that keep us spinning round and round in the old reality trap. This trap that tells us that things just happen to us and sometimes we cannot change it no matter how much we seem to try to. This is a trap because of the backwards steps it can lead us spinning round and round in old reality we no longer prefer. But we can also use it as an opportunity to really see what it is we are focusing on or how our own energy is leading us astray.

Let us use an example of something you really wanted and you have been focusing on it and every time the thought of that desire comes up you think of already having it, it is all good vibes. Yet a few weeks, months or more have gone by and still your desire is not fulfilled and you know you have been doing better then the best you have ever done. Even if you kept up the feeling good vibrations longer and longer more then ever in your past and yet still no manifestation into physical for you then the next thing you realize is that you are starting to fall into hopelessness. The old pattern seems to come upon you so quickly and easily that all it took was a little bit of thoughts of doubt and then that lead to giving up. Sometimes that's what it takes to let go, surrender. By giving up even out of frustration, you are still letting go, not caring any longer. Which allows yourself to be in the state of being of allowing your desire to manifest. But if we continue after the letting go to again focus on the doubts then we are spinning our webs again of canceling our manifestations too.

The contrast to the high feelings of the orgasmic way have all tumbled into a hopeless despaired feelings to even give up on your desire once and for all. When many times that is usually when we are closer then ever but do not realize it to your fulfilled desire. In other words, it is just around the corner. The old emotional addiction seems to creep in and before you realize it you are feeling so down about it and your day just continues to unfold in that downward swirl. You feel like the creator or guides or universe is not on your side or out having lunch or something and not helping you. This is the trick of the old addictions of emotions and beliefs from the past that is really sneaking through. Most times it can go unnoticed and is the reason we think we have done all we could in our focusing and yet no desire manifested. It can make us believe that something other then our own self has done this to us because we sure wouldn't create this kind of experience.

This is where the spinning round and round will keep us locked into that path until we take our power back by realizing it had to be our own self and no one else. All the blaming, anger and frustration will do is keep us spinning until we eventually become ill to not feeling well, that is where that path will always lead to.

Nothing will change until we use our awareness on what there is to show us of what lead to this depressed feeling state. We must come to the realization that somewhere along our thoughts of beliefs we detoured and did not notice how the ripple effect was flowing. When we finally realize we do not feel so good about anything and have that kind of day with awareness, we'll know.

Sure we can do something that will lift us out of that depressed feeling however if we don't cut the ties of the old ways then we will keep repeating the old way. Whether it is by using blame or other victim thoughts until we severe those bonds when things do not go as we want others or anything to be. We must come to realize and know that it is always our own self that creates it all to begin with, this is giving ourselves the opportunity to know ourselves until we get it right on. If we are not manifesting what we want then we have more fine tuning of our own self to know where we make those detours to begin with.

Continually Returning to Our Own Self

This is taking all of our responsibility for how and what we were thinking that created our self not to manifest our desire. We must always return to our own self to know our self in every thing we think, say and do because we will see the proof when we realize it. Also realize it is important not to stay focused in it for too long because it will keep the detour going in the same direction. Instead be aware that it had to be our own self that created it and it is up to our own self to get unstuck and back to feeling good again.

That is how we finally get unstuck from the muck and chaos that we have created to be broken apart to recreate again. Placing no judgments on ourselves but only awareness. This keeps us returning to our own self, knowing we are doing everything to our own self all of the time, which is simultaneously taking our own power back too. Remember what the orgasmic experience of feelings feels like or felt like and desire to get back to that feeling again and again to keep the creating in the vibration that you desire to manifest.

All the detours are also creating whether you are aware of it or not is still creating more of what you do not want just because you choose to play in the muck for the good old not good feelings. If you take notice you will see the detours creating your reality too.

It is stopping the falling down process to become more habitual to less and less of falling into it to begin so we can stop the spinning wheel of thought to jump off it and realize that we are still creating in that mood. Remember without judging our selves and instead just jump off that spinning wheel of thought consciously whenever we first start to feel the fall coming. We are aware and stop it in the process before it escalates to fall from the wisdom that it is our own self choosing the doubtful, depressed thoughts to begin with, not anyone or anything else. Then we are not creating the things we do not want along the way that will only create more for us to undo to recreate. This is how we stop the spinning round and round of the old reality trap to ease through to our manifestation. To keep using the orgasmic feelings to guide us along our way.

CHAPTER 11

LET ORGASM BE YOUR GUIDE

When we allow our minds to wonder about ideas we expand our curiosity to know more. Most of the time new expanding ideas are the ones that can transform our old beliefs so that we can create more beneficial beliefs. Letting orgasm be your guide is one of those expanding higher benefits of wisdom. Then we can expand to ask ourselves, can the orgasmic state be our guide for everything?

Awareness for Everything

Really give some in depth thought to this because it may really open your eyes to what is going on. The media can condition us with suggestions concerning everything from our health to what we eat to brushing our teeth. It can be such a fine line that most of the time goes without noticing even for many of us on the awakening path.

The only way to know for sure is to question almost everything you do and why you do it that will bring much awareness to why you do what you do. Even to the most simplistic act of brushing our teeth and what tooth paste we use, if we gargle or not, and even how we use the brush on our teeth.

Beliefs are so intricately interwoven into our daily lives seem to go unnoticed because they have become such automatic reactions to doing the things we do, habitually. By questioning these things allow us to delve further into ourselves and choose to do things differently just because we desire to. When we desire to break the habitual automatic way we do things to realize that most of it has been subconsciously suggested to us from not our real natural creative orgasmic self.

So where did you even get the notion that you had to brush your teeth to begin with? Hmm good question. You may have not given any thought to it and assumed you did it just because it was your choice. Quite the fine line how we have been conditioned with suggestions in doing so much of what we do.

It is empowering when we become more aware by noticing and start questioning these things, instead of letting the media be our authority, because it will always appear as if we have no power. For myself for over twenty years I have allowed my body and have been my own authority regardless of what the pain or body reaction is. If there is pain in any area of my body, I keep my focus on what the message is from my own body's communication.

Also take into consideration that just because I am writing this book does not mean that I have it all under control either, but every day in every way I continue to be aware as much as I can. Just as many authors or teacher will also share what they are learning from experiences as they go along.

Working on being our own authority expands our consciousness to know and courageously move forward to the next experiences of alignment of evolving. It is what we are doing to be able to use more of our latent power that is sitting there waiting for us to do just that, to live an orgasmic life.

So be bold, go where the bold go, unfold into the unknowing to know, starting with our own selves, questioning everything big and small to know who is really in control. Through the process it allows us to connect with our creative flow and amazing ideas will always present themselves. Of course we do not have to get so wound up in everything however the more we do the more we will learn about ourselves.

Another example is why do we watch the news if we do watch the news? Many have stopped it as entertainment, realizing that it only triggers more fear tactics by perpetuating the conditioning of suggestions. Always asking how does it make you feel is a great indicator of the automatic reactions it triggers and also if it really does not feel good then why do it. Unless of course it has become an automatic habit to feel bad from years of getting too comfortable in those negative feelings.

Remember **it only takes an instant** every once in awhile to realize how you are feeling about something and changing the automatic thoughts to a more orgasmic one. Instantly we can change our mind about the things that we are doing so robotically.

For example watching the news, what if you are at someone else's home and they put on the news, instead of arguing or creating a stir about it we can use it as our own opportunity to observe how we respond. The opportunity is our teacher to reflect and bring our response to an orgasmic state of being, that way it will be filled with purposeful benefits.

Also keep in mind if something is already on a pleasurable path as the example of brushing our teeth, if we choose to brush our teeth even regardless of it being a habitual suggestion . We can take that into consideration that it is also our own choice to continue that action but now with awareness of it being our own choice. It can be regarded as a good choice in alignment with what we are already doing anyway without any resistance.

So now in comparison to creating a new belief that we do not have to brush our teeth to have healthy and clean teeth. That would be using more resistance to something that is already working for us but now with the awareness that we now know we are choosing it. Even though it was a suggestion originally from somewhere else. Which we can do with everything when we take notice or question many of the things we do.

For myself and probably you too, congratulate yourself, we are stretching or expanding to be out of the normal range of desires as a way to test our own abilities and how far we really can go.

So it is in the joy and excitement of experimenting and being able to do new things from a creative orgasmic source instead of dictated control norm way that everyone else thinks it should be. From the result of someone who we were told had more authority over us then our own selves. Evolving is breaking free from those old limiting conditioned beliefs and trusting in the wisdom from our own experiences that we can ultimately be our own authorities.

All we have to do is take notice of all the new diseases that 'they" are trying to suggest while conditioning people, and then create the cures as they do with flu shots. The best way is to ask yourself the questions and then feel the reply from your own heart felt feelings to know if you resonate with it. Be your own guide by how you feel about the question and the true heart felt answer will also come. You will either resonate with it or not, then you will know for absolute, you will, without any doubts.

That is what the wisdom of knowing is, and that is being true to one's own self, that is being our own authority.

So back to the new diseases that are being creating to be a problem, one I heard of is shyness. Well for most of us on our awakened path we know what shyness stems from, simply lack of self esteem in our own confidence to trust our own self to begin with. It is giving the power away to believe that others are more important and know more then we do. It is taking that power back that will cure shyness. Whoever they who are decided to label it as a disease that they then created a pharmaceutical pill or medication to take for it.

The list goes on too far with these types of conditioning suggestions. They usually are from authorities who either know how to hypnotize people through conditioning to do what they want them to do, or if they don't, either way we can just send love as that's the most beneficial response. Keeping our energy in an orgasmic state of being so that we respond of the highest potential for all.

To be powerless and never even think of something as powerful as a cure to own one self and our own authority? "They" do not want us to do that because who would they have left to control? Who would they have to be an authority to?

When we become to know how our body works and how it responds we then know that all disease is only an attention getter to get our self back to the harmonious state of our divine orgasmic self.

This is a big quantum leap of a jump for all the other things we have become so enslaved by conditioning from other authorities and finally desire orgasmically, excitedly to do what we need to do to take our power back. It becomes such a fun filled, ecstatic path to follow and the rewards go naturally hand in hand. So there are so many benefits in the leading edge. Be a leading edge surfer and you will be so surprised that you will be in the orgasmic state of being more and more.

CHAPTER 12

THE PLAYGROUND OF ORGASM'S ECSTASY

As I am writing this chapter, I find it to be the most exciting and fun chapter to write about because we can now really delve into the really outrageous possibilities that can flow from our creative infinite orgasmic source. And believe it or not, it is even becoming more challenging to find extraordinary things to do that has not already been done.

It is becoming more and more known that it is not what we put into our mouths that creates our body to become, it is what we think about what we put in our mouths. It is the thinking, the meaning, the definition that creates the expectation of what the body cells will do with the information, or commands for it to do. So by realizing that nothing matters but what we think about anything is what creates it to be.

Some individuals can eat very little amounts of food and stay overweight, while others can eat everything and still be slim. The reason is because of what they think about what they are eating, which creates their metabolism to create the body cells to create it to react. Even though many of these individuals may not even realize this is what they are doing and what is being created.

For years I ate whatever I wanted, others would ask me how I can eat so much and sustain my weight and not gain extra pounds. Just as I explained in the other chapter about taking any junk food that normal beliefs create as unhealthy over weight body. I think to create beliefs that will support the idea that everything I put into my system is good for me. Now my beliefs automatically creates whatever I put in my mouth to turn automatically into nutritional commands for my body cells. I have been doing this for so long it is just a fantastic simple orgasmic natural habit now.

I listened to my own authority and would not alter it for no other who would claim to know more then I did about my own body, especially when it works that way for me. How can anyone else dictate what we choose to think about our own bodies or brain or spirit. When you turn to knowing your own self and trusting that knowing then no one else ever can burst your bubble and that is being in the orgasmic state of being, the playground of ecstatic infinity.

I have done the same thing through menopause, no doctor or getting any medical advice or medication through any of it.

It keeps me in the orgasmic state of evolving to more unknown dimensions and realities that the orgasmic path of living will guide me to.

How about for you?

Many of you reading this book probably have already done so much of what I am writing about, but there may be many who are curious but may never desire to experience these things. Others may just be too skeptical and only take whatever they resonate with and may have stopped reading this book after the first chapter?

It does not matter, nothing matters except for what you desire for it to matter. It is my intention to share what I have experienced and that is all because everything is left up to each individual on their own free will path.

Just by realizing the real power of the wisdom that if there is nothing that is not impossible, then everything is possible, then what is left that we cannot do?

Its unlimited, infinite to choose and that is mind boggling in itself. So think about it, expand into your creative source and allow desires to surface of what would be quite amazing. Not only to entertain the imaginings that surface but also the possibilities of being able to one day really experience the most seeming impossible ideas that come up now.

Would that not be quite the orgasmic feeling?

It is our highest potential to remind our self that nothing is too big or too small to create when it comes to creation. It is only our own beliefs of what we believe to be possible or impossible.

Reversing the aging process to a desired age, mine is 35 years young and sustaining it. What is your desired reversal age? If you have not created an age to reverse to then the body will continue to react to the aging beliefs. Its focusing on the desire and expecting it and the cells are always picking up on your thoughts and responds.

Eyesight Experiment

How about perfect eyesight when your eyes start deteriorating only because of a limiting old belief, but once aware and create the new wisdom, we become to see perfectly without those magnifying glasses. It also goes along with a 35 year young healthy body too, everything will readjust to the desire in a flowing way.

To share an amazing experience with you that I experimented with my eye sight. Before I knew about the knowledge of the body and brain I did unconsciously allow myself to be conditioned to aging. However once I took the knowledge I was learning and experimented enough so that it became my own proof, which became my present wisdom of it all. So when my eye sight started to deteriorate to not be able to see up close unless I used magnifying glasses, which I did use for years. Then I started to experiment by giving myself new suggestions in an orgasmical blissful state.

I started with writing out affirmations, as that helps ingrain it better to sketch it into my brain of thoughts of memory. I would hold up writing that was all blurred. Then I would imagine the blurred writing become magnified just as my glasses would do but without the glasses. I did that for a couple of days and then the next day the blur automatically became so clear as if I had my glasses on. I continued to do that because I knew I had to form the successful memory of it for future retrievals to be able to continue seeing it that way. I was so amazed because it became on command when I focused on any blurred writing and it would become normal vision to see it clearly. Then I would notice that I was not able to do it when I was not focusing on doing it and expecting it. Again it takes practice, to the point that whenever I stare and bring up the retrieved memory of doing it the first few times, whatever I am viewing then automatically becomes clear.

I also experienced many times while I was reading a book and certain lines would highlight to colors that were illuminating as colored lights. The color yellow or white and green would be so illuminating of a bright light on and off as I continued to read.

The possibilities are endless and when we allow ourselves to delve into that stream of infinite consciousness, that creative flow, that orgasmic heavenly bliss we will be living heaven on earth in our physical bodies. We will be the spiritual beings in our physical bodies with awareness of who we really are, our natural unlimited selves, all for the experience to experience it in physical reality.

So big cheers to unlimited imaginings while being in the orgasmic state of being.

CHAPTER 13

\ \

ORGASMIC DAYS IN EVERY WAY

EVERYTHING IS SEEN LOVINGLY

Everything does start to change because we can never go back when we have expanded our consciousness into newer realms of possibilities.

You may find you are no longer interested in babbling talks of uninteresting conversations. You may find you no longer turn on the television unless it is something that you can learn or maybe for a relief to laugh or something really interesting.

You are never ever bored because it has become just a natural state of flow of creativity and there is so many things you are practicing, learning or experiencing.

You see everyone and everything in a different perception and as a reflection that continuously keeps you learning about yourself. When another says anything that in the past would anger or irritate you, you would automatically get upset over, now you just smile, because orgasmic feelings has overflowed into everything. You no longer ever desire to alter from your orgasmic bliss reality even when someone or something triggers you to react as in the past. It only takes us a second to get back to orgasmic bliss because it just feels so heavenly good and has become a natural habit.

Sunsets and sunrises are spectacular and you try to never miss one. You notice how unique every sunset or sunrise is. You also notice that every time you look to the sky it is always in a different unique state. You just sit and revel at the beauty of its awesome changes while you observe and you create and see the clouds form into whatever shape you choose.

Your first cup of coffee smells and taste like heaven, bringing blissful orgasm to your sensations, every cup becomes to do that, also with everything you eat or drink.

It becomes this way with everything and anything, it is a more heavenly experience, blended with uniqueness, you look forward to it all. Sensations of flavor of foods and drinks are so intensified, it is as if the textures are all new with new sensations. Your kids, lover, friends all take on a new glow, regardless of what they are speaking or saying, it is all a slow motion of bliss, orgasm has flowed into your daily life in all ways.

All chores are no longer chores but have an orgasmic flow in how you do them and in how they feel when you are doing them. You never feel rushed or the old feeling of stress of what you have to do or should do. You do what you want when you want, it is all in your own flow and choosing.

You feel more energized every day, and your body feels healthily renewed all of the time. You walk by a mirror and smile and say, hey I really do love you and the mirror reflects it back with such genuine love with heart felt feelings. And those heart felt feelings flow into everyone you encounter and every experience you experience. You leave ten to fifteen minutes earlier then your normal time, just for the extra relaxation of getting there in flow, in a relaxed state instead of a rushed stressed state. You see more then you have ever noticed on any road you take, even on the same daily road you travel, you become aware of more new things.

Sounds become amplified yet in a soft vibration. You notice how you easily become one with so many things during your daily experiences. Stars in the night sky become so alive and you feel as if you can rename then so easily with your own flavor through the experience of observing them. You even wonder and know you have created some of them just by your explosion of orgasmic thoughts and feelings, exploding new stars in the appearing heavens of the skies.

You notice more friendly, smiling relaxed individuals that are also happily flowing along with their day. You stop to talk to the birds that are having such fun brushing themselves in the dirt, and they actual look at you and continue their pleasure, as if knowing your actually communicating and smiling with them.

You have become luckier, even though you know that luck is an illusion, really it is your high vibration of energy that keeps you in the frequency of being in the heavenly experiences. Almost every lottery ticket you buy is a winner in small ways that become bigger each week.

You feel lighter and more lifted, almost as if you are singing and dancing along each day. You notice that you rarely ever meet up with rushed angry drivers as you did in the past. You pick up so easily now from higher vibrations, from your infinite higher self, from multiple guides, spirits from other dimensions.

You may even have started your own dictionary of new words to describes these new feeling experiences that the norm dictionary can never describe. So to describe it into verbal it just flows out outrageously into feel good words like **lumpiously orgnicimis.** Those words just came out right now to describe my incredible feeling I am having presently, but incredible does not do it justice to explaining clearly what I am feeling, yet the creative word that came out does.

You get such an orgasmic feeling when you bend metal with only your intention and energy, no physical touch, all in the energy of being one with the metal object. You barely notice the clocks but when you do you are always surprise how fast the time went by. When you go for a walk you take in such amplified feelings through your senses.

If wealth of money has still not flowed in multiples to you yet, when you open a bill you are not able to pay, you feel no stress as you did in the past because you know that the INFINITE OF CREATION will bring it to you, it always does since you have been in this flow of allowing.

You become to really appreciate what you are doing is what you love to do and multiple sources of money comes in flow as a result. All stress seemed to evaporate back into the ethers with no desire to ever have it return, because orgasmic blissful living has saturated your life and you could not ever go back. It would be similar to going back to kindergarten as a full grown adult as a student not a teacher, no one would ever do that.

It is the same type of experience once we become accustom to living a blissful orgasmic life, heaven, trust are all natural qualities that go hand in hand with it.

Telepathy is always occurring and synchronicity is our natural flow. We come to know that all desires we have were always there created in the instantaneous moment we desired them in our imagining. We realized it was only our own self that got in the way of our desires being instantaneously manifested to our self. We were manifesting what we expected which was to wait, to expect it within whatever we believed from old beliefs of how long was sufficient for us to wait for the manifestations. It became through hindsight an orgasmic learning experience that becomes our new wisdom through our experiences. Then we can imagine to manifest instantly when we desire when that knowledge has become our wisdom.

All loving appreciation for everything also becomes part of the parcel. We cannot help but appreciate when we are in this heavenly state, everything is genuinely appreciated with love from our natural heart felt state of being. We expand in our orgasmic heavenliness to desire more unknown possibilities just because it is contained in infinite source.

So from this state of being we only can expand further and farther, as our desires are more expansive and enjoyable. What our focus of attention becomes is wrapped in orgasmic bliss in every way within every day. There is nothing that we cannot do because everything is possible when we know it is. It is in that knowing that we are continuously creating and that is the way it has always been. The only difference now is that we know, **heavenly bliss was only a thought away** always awaiting for us to connect it into our daily lives. In every way, every day through the hidden key that orgasm reveals to live life blissfully.

CHAPTER 14

SEXUALITY SEEMS TO BE IN EVERYTHING

Everything seems to be about arousal and sex, have you noticed? It is in songs, movies, commercials, in everything. Many may be against it all occurring because of the old attached thoughts about it trying to consume everything in a negative way. This is important because we must get passed the ego. We must get past all those limiting ways of perceiving and judging what is going on now and how it just may be for a higher beneficial purpose in our future.

If we use an analogy of a puzzle, it is until all the pieces of a puzzle are put together when we can see the whole picture and make sense of it.

So there may be a very spiritual reason for all that is going on presently that sex or sensuality is seeming to consume into everything we see and hear for the past few decades and presently. It is to allow ourselves to expand further to realize what the heaven is going on and the reasons for it.

To see beyond the pieces of it just becoming a sensual sexual world to expanding into what it is to become in our future. Which is to let go of all the limiting attachments and bring it to its full blown conception. Bring it right out into the open of what may be originally of its unfolding blueprint to unravel for our future potentials. Remove all the tainted old beliefs that we may have with sex and sensuality.

Sensuality is a feeling and it does seem to be the most intense feeling there is and it is connected in orgasm. Which we have come to realize that this heavenly feeling we are in is the same feeling when we have orgasm. So this is where we must expand our minds to become to realize that all that is going on with our sexual revolution is to do just that, bring it out into the open. By doing that we become to feel more comfortable with it in everything, because it is everywhere we look. And when we perceive it with the divine or heavenly intention the way will be paved with golden wisdom of exuberance beyond the illusions of past beliefs. When we are willing to do this it can become into this present now by practicing and taking it in the proper content it may have been originally formatted of a higher purpose.

It can never be over stated to come to this simple realization to bring us to knowing of the wisdom it holds. Which is to own the experience of it into our daily lives so that we can live a blissful paradise of our lives in every way, everyday. So we can once and for all not need the use of pharmaceutical medicated drugs, or recreational drugs, or alcohol or anything other then what orgasm was originally designed to do for us.

Now remember I am not saying that we cannot use our power by what meaning we give to everything that is originally neutral to begin with. Yes we can do that because after enough experience we then know that it is about what we think about what we digest or put into our bodies. It is the thought that only matters that will create the body to respond as in the way we think it to respond.

What is of importance here is the not knowing that this is the way it works, for the individuals who are using the external things to bring what orgasmic living can bring instead. It is the wisdom to know this and release in that knowing that all can come as a result from what orgasm shows us to use it for, more then just a fleeting moment of ecstasy. And to bring it in every way into everything we do in our daily lives. The temptation being in not using orgasm and instead being tempted by anything other then what sexuality is evolving as a collective consciousness in leading to resolve.

When we come to see the whole picture of how the explosion of sensuality is in all of our lives in everything now, is the triggering to expand that wisdom and allow its flow. Because eventually this notion and what this book is all about will bring the realization that the original inspiration is to grow orgasmically to create our lives in heaven's bliss.

Once all the negative judgment are released with sensuality and brought back into harmony of its original intentions for our future, it will then be recognized and fulfilled from that point onward. It won't be shamed or criticized or ignored for its content, it will be expanded into the loving intentional pieces it was always there to show us. It will evolve into the higher love that has been enticing us all along, to bring it to full penetration collectively and evolve to the divinity of it, true love of it, true Source of it All.

Let us expand into a future vision of reality as if collectively we have already evolved to get a glimpse of a future world. When all the pieces were put together to acknowledge what a world like that would be.

The whole population of the planet would never become ill or diseased because they are living an orgasmic life as a result of being in an orgasmic state of being. There would be no violence because everyone would know and own their ecstasy feeling and be living it daily, peaceful harmony would be the result. So there would be no more medical anything. No hospitals, no drugs of any kind, no doctors, no healers, everyone would be healthy as a result of their own sovereignty of blissful orgasm living. Because anyone who is orgasmically living life that way cannot get sick. It is impossible when we are in that state of being all of the time, the bodies cells are then perpetually in harmony.

No one would age, we would experience eternal being in physical because in that orgasmic state of living and being, we become ageless and timeless.

Everything is just blissful in everything we do. Everyone would love what they are doing as a service for monetary receivership, money may not even be what we use any longer. We may just circulate our returning services to each other instead.

So much power is in that orgasmic state of being and living that we know we effect everything externally. And because we are so aligned with the infinite source, everything that is objectively connected to us works in perfect harmony too. That means vehicle, appliances, computers, everything.

There would be no secrets because telepathy would be brought out into the open, everyone would be using it, as a result everything is simultaneously accepted. We become sovereign beings. No insurances, or big companies, because there is no more greedy control or influence, everything is shared.

The possibilities are really endless and one could really go into specific depths of how the future world would be, and for many of us, we already know that we are on our way to that right now. We are in the process as so many things are transforming to bring us to that reality. This is what the Mayan's were referring to with the shift of our planet in transforming it to an expanded, evolved loving consciousness to experience in physical.

It can be acknowledged as we find the hidden key that orgasm was originally intended for all of this to be expanded as a result. So orgasmic living is what our future is becoming, and all that is going on presently may have a golden lining to it all. And all the pieces may be reminders of how it is transforming to eventually become.

So orgasm is the doorway to our future.

Orgasm is where all the power is and where we must expand to living life orgasmically.

We can then be of the wisdom that orgasm is the most important state of being, thing, experience to transforming, shifting ourselves and collectively bringing consciousness to that evolved reality. It is in the process of happening now and has been for decades.

CHAPTER 15

` ` ` ` ` ` ` ` ` ` ` ` ` ` ` ` ` `

QUANTUM PHYSIC'S ORGASM TENDENCY'S

It seems that the majority of humanity has missed the realizing of wisdom of what ancient cultures and masters were showing us all along. What most religions left out and quantum physics came through because we continually kept missing the wisdom, the data of information of the nature of reality. As we are becoming to realize through experiments and experiences that guides us to turn to our own wisdom that the Creator is within us and orgasm is too. Always leading and urging us to expand what the limited mind of beliefs continuously kept missing, of where creation and heaven through orgasm has been to show us the way to live it in physical.

Quantum physics shows us that all is possible. That we can pick any desire of infinite possibilities and that we can create it when we let go of old beliefs that have limited us, then we can take notice of its validity.

Quantum physics also shows us that when we observe anything and it is dependant on the meaning we define it that creates the observation to become what we expect it to become.

Quantum physics lead us to take advantage of what quantum states are all about, we must expand our minds our consciousness to comprehend what quantum is showing us. Quantum physics shows us that we are not one solid physical being with one physical body and life that we are multidimensional beings. Quantum physics shows us that we have abilities that are so powerful, that we are powerful and can create and experience things that once seemed impossible.

Quantum physics is showing us that all we believed to be science fiction is now becoming factual. All that was once perceived as weird in the paranormal phenomenal is now not only being more accepted but is actually becoming disciplines to practice to use more of our Creator's creative abilities. Quantum physics shows us through entanglement that we are all one, all connected, unified from one Source, one vibration frequency field that sustains all, infinitely.

So we can see that quantum physics has opened the way for us to expand to know more about reality and our own selves. I think it came upon through science because we continually kept missing the signs that ancient traditions and the orgasmic state were always there to show us.

It seems that quantum physics came about in our discovery because we kept missing the mark to know more. When orgasm was there all along, to remind humanity of a remembering, as an awakening to what reality and heavenly bliss is all about. Since we still did not get it, or missed the signs to realize, then quantum physics had to pop up to show us the way back to what orgasm was always there to show us to begin with.

Orgasm shows us if we were to expand to stay in it longer that we would then find the other doors, other dimensions that are there to discover.

Though there are many tools also to get us there, as meditation, imagination, they are all the same as orgasm, the only difference is that orgasm is a more pleasurable tool. The detour always has been that most of us only used orgasm as a tool for one thing when it is a multidimensional tool that can lead us to the best feeling good state all of the time.

To bask in it as long as we can until we become so habitually comfortable that we reverse the polarity of our old habitual of not good feelings to become the desire to want to feel it all the time. Then the not good feeling is then a reminder that we just stepped out of the orgasmic feeling and the desire returns to quickly get back into it. As a reminder that our health also depends on it, actually everything in every potential way in our lives depends on it for our expanding evolving growth.

When we can see more of the expanded picture of reality, it is like putting so many pieces together to realize how it all fits in so perfectly, to use all the tools that evolves us to heavenly bliss on earth.

CHAPTER 16

\` \` \` \` \` \` \` \` \` \` \` \` \` \` \` \` \` \` \`

THE IMPORTANCE OF LETTING GO

How important is wanting or desiring something, anything, everything that we do want in our lives?

Have we had enough experiences of contrast, oppositions and resistance? Enough experiences of what we no longer want and we can now know what we want because whatever makes us feel so good is what we should be living and experiencing in our lives. Not just sometimes but all of the time.

If we are not blissful in our days then we know we are not living the life we truly desire and it will lead most of us to make changes whether we realize those changes are enfolding to have life the way we want. Some may never reach that high and just accept the life they really do not want and sacrifice orgasmic bliss for it out of habit from old beliefs. The importance is when we do know what we want and we find out that we can have anything we ever wanted, that nothing is impossible and we are deserving of it all.

To know that our Infinite Creator has always wanted us to know, for us to extend our trust to that exuberant knowledge and turn it into wisdom.

This is where orgasm can show us how to do just that by taking a closer look at orgasm itself. We have fun and pleasure up until the release into orgasm, but the most blissful, heavenly feeling to experience is when we really let go. Irrelevant of what it takes us to get to that point, it is in the letting go, the release that we arrive to feel the most ecstatic experience to feel, orgasmic bliss.

If we have never experienced orgasm before or it took many years to finally reach it or whatever life of old beliefs that kept us from that experience, once we did experience it, experiences of sex changes.

It is like the end point to a new beginning of what a most blissful feeling of experience then is, it is no longer just a sexual experience it is always choosing to feel that orgasm again.

The important thing here to realize that it is in the LETTING GO, the RELEASE that brings us the most fantastic heavenly experience. It is as if the Creator put it there so we could easily find its meaning.

Letting go is the most important step also to creating our desires to manifest for us. To be in the receivership of accepting it for ourselves in physical reality to experience. So no matter what our desire is, we can focus and put our attention on it and visualize it as it is already ours with feelings and excitement. But it will never manifest until we release with the letting go of it. Knowing it is released into the invisible realm to come back to us like a boomerang. Even if the boomerang doesn't come back for days, months, years or eons, it seems whenever a seed is planted in some time in space the manifestation of it will eventually appear if we are aware to notice it.

Let us go back to recalling our experiences with orgasm. It is until we let go, let the release come forward to experience orgasm, if we never let go we would not experience it. So orgasm has always showed us the hidden key to creating because it is in the letting go that we trust we are going to manifest our desire. Or when we let go out of desperation of just giving up because we tried everything and still no manifestation. No matter what way we let go it will always be the key to the releasing for whatever our desire will be manifested. Anything before that letting go part is still in a process of getting us to letting go. This also true even when we are unaware creators too, the difference is no awareness of what's going on.

We can stay in that in between state for a long time, it is dependant on when we finally let go that we then release the power for it to manifest. And we must trust that it will. We may have sex and not have orgasm and when that happens it is because we did not put ourselves into the moment fully. If we are worrying about our bills or our family or anything else then that's what we are doing in those moments while in the sexual act then we experience sex with no orgasm. Which is the same as having a desire but not being passionate present with it to the point for it to unfold in leading us to orgasm, to having it manifested.

When we can visualize and imagine our desires as if we are already experiencing it our imagination as if we are living it for real subjectively then we have planted the seed. We then feel assured and feel good about it and doubt dissolves. That is the trust, the feeling good of it. You are playing with it in your mind as if it was already yours and then you let it go, releasing it from your attention or concentration. Just as you experienced your orgasm in sex, you fore played, let go and released and feel so high and blissful after it.

The same thing when you let go of your focus on your desire as it already is, you do the same thing, let go and release and feel good about it like you did when you just experienced your orgasm. After that everything looks brighter and is magnified of its beauty, everything. Then you extend that great feeling no matter what comes up to challenge or test you. Passing the test so to speak for yourself is not falling back to the old ways that do not allow you the good feelings.

When we continuously encounter everything with that orgasmic blissful feeling, it transforms everything in your path and paves the days to continue to unfold that way all day long.

Keep reminding yourself, do I want to stay blissful or fall back to humdrum low energies?

Especially when knowing you are really letting go all day long if you desire to keep feeling good all day long without perpetually falling downwards until you then realized how depressed you feel. Who created those feelings? You did by reacting the old ways, choosing not to respond orgasmically, the way heavenly bliss would. Remember it is always our own self that alters us from our orgasmic blissful state, not what we think others can do to us.

Who is in the power seat, you or another or a situation? Let it all go and keep the focus on the orgasmic feelings and that will always return us back to bliss.

Let go, release, let go, release, let go and release, that can be a new empowering mantra to keep the reminder present. Knowing it is up to ourselves to let go of everything of old meanings and give it the orgasmic definition that then allows it to have meaning for our potential and sustains our orgasmic blissful heavenly experiences. To live a expinluminusary life by keeping our feelings generated from the most orgasmic thinking.

CHAPTER 17

ORGASMIC INSPIRATION COMPARED TO MOTIVATION

We can again compare foreplay as motivation and orgasm as inspiration when it comes to comparing the differences of inspiration versus motivation.

Motivation compared to foreplay can still be fun, however it's not going to be the ultimate experience of orgasm as inspiration is. We become motivated to move in a certain direction when we are desiring something we want and then accomplishing our goals. However motivation can become draining as we continue to keep our self to stay motivated until we accomplish our goals.

Inspiration actually does the opposite of motivation. Inspiration contains a passion that is a high vibration of frequency, so instead of pushing along as we do in motivation, when we are in inspiration we have more energy. We feel lifted and ideas come through to us so easily, in a constant flow as we constantly feel refreshed as inspiration has its natural flow of being in-spired.

Just as we work through foreplay as in motivation to get us to our goal of orgasm. Or if we playfully go through foreplay as inspiration to get us to orgasm, it is always the prize that the experience or orgasm gives us. So there is again different ways to experience orgasm, a journey of rough roads or a journey of easy fun roads. Orgasm is the experience in the higher vibrations.

When we experience orgasm we feel so light, refreshed and it is like seeing through loving heavenly lens of perception. We are inspired because we just experienced the highest of dimension that orgasm is, a state of being that is of its ultimate infinite realm.

It seems that males love to relax or sleep after orgasm, they feel so content and full of love and pleasure. Many females become more energized after orgasm as it regenerate their energy level. Whatever you do after the experience of orgasm I am quite sure you would agree that you feel uplifted and loving.

I know I am mentioning it again that it is when we remember and continue in that orgasmic feeling into everything we continue to do when we really start to experiencing living so blissfully orgasmically regardless of what's going on. The benefits will over flow into everything with inspiration leading the way.

CHAPTER 18

TRANSMUTING ORGASM

The first time I ever heard of sexual transmuting was a couple of decades ago in Napoleon Hill's book, "Think and Grow Rich with Peace of Mind."

As I have already stated in the beginning of this book how I wondered and pondered since my first orgasm about what seemed as a mysteriously magical purposeful key. The hidden key that the Infinite Creator created orgasm as the key to opening us to know more about ourselves and reality.

It was through Napoleon Hill's book I found so many answers about sexual transmutation. Of how the arousing feelings of sexual stimuli, and instead of letting go into the release of orgasm we keep our self sustained in it. Which is what sexual transmutation is, when we stay in that heightened sensual arousal state of being and allow our highest creativity to flow out into whatever we are doing, except without letting go into orgasm or climaxing.

So I have taken it a step further through my own experimenting that created the experiences that I have shared throughout this book. That we don't have to stay in the sustained foreplay of the arousing stimuli and instead let go into the orgasmic state and keep that memory of the orgasmic experience and over flow it into everything we do. It is being in the orgasmic state all day long, feeling light, free and loving through everything.

Orgasmic transmutation is simply living by experiencing our life consciously in the most orgasmic blissful ways. We come to know that feeling orgasmically great and perpetuate that orgasmic feeling high all day long is transmuting orgasmic feelings of experiences into every single thing we do. Even though it may take repetitious practice to not only convince ourselves that this is the infinite way, but also because of all the natural benefits. Just an any habit we have created from past repetition we finally break free from and continue on our desires for the changes. Orgasmic transmutation will eventually become our natural way to be, do and experience everything.

Through enough experiences when we do alter from our natural orgasmic blissful transmutational state, we will feel the discord. We will feel the disharmony, the out of natural orgasmic rhythm, and that will be enough that will create our desire to continue in the blissful state. Because altering from that magnificent state will become to feel too painful, too disharmonize in comparison, and orgasmic bliss will sustain a constant consistent urging to keep us in its amazing beneficial feelings.

It is then that you know you have not only found the hidden key but have also used the key to unlock the universal infinite wisdom that orgasmic transmutation so naturally desired you to find. Then you will wonder how you may have missed the wisdom to begin with. However that becomes unimportant because once you know and experience it enough, it becomes the only way for you. Your daily experiences will reflect it so naturally. It will embed so naturally in experiencing everything with the greatest appreciation, even all the once perceived challenges will transform into orgasmic blissful ecstatic living. So then you found the hidden key and you used the key and never have to search for it again.

CHAPTER 19

ˎ ˎ ˎ ˎ ˎ ˎ ˎ ˎ ˎ ˎ ˎ ˎ ˎ ˎ ˎ ˎ ˎ ˎ

ORGASM'S NATURAL APPRECIATION

Orgasm contains all the high vibrational radiant magnetism frequencies and appreciation is another one of those high energy states that we naturally find as we live our life through and in orgasm ways.

It is taught that gratitude is a lower vibration because when we are grateful there is still a missing piece that appreciation fills in. Gratitude can keeps us in a lingering state that has us believing we should be grateful for a reason. Appreciation contains the high vibration of being appreciative because of its natural free flowing ability through orgasmic bliss. Having no reasons like gratitude does, instead it is contained in the expansion of orgasm's frequency.

Just as in the chapter of inspiration compared to motivation, when we allow ourselves to be wise to the different vibrations we feel the evidence. Inspiration just as appreciation is from the orgasmic vibration and motivation just as gratitude has some intermingled ego energy contained. When we feel grateful we still feel a reason for our gratitude, like a need for our gratefulness.

However when we feel appreciative we feel no need, no reason, we just bask in the appreciative light that is seeded in appreciation. We are not grateful for anything in appreciation, we just naturally appreciate because it feels so good in everything when we feel it in our heart and being.

Try it right now to experience it for yourself. Look at anything, right now and say out loud, I am so grateful for whatever it is your are focused upon. Now say out loud as you focus on what you have picked, I feel so appreciative.

Did you feel a difference? If not try it again, you will feel the difference. One can be felt to be lighter in nature then the other. It's these subtle noticing in the moments of awareness that allows us to not only see but feel the differences in orgasmic vibration compared to ego vibrations. This really is what creates our lives to be more infinitely orgasmic in every way. You will then notice that the natural orgasmic nature of appreciation will shine to radiant everything throughout your day. That will overflow into your sleep and dreams into an overflow of everything and everyone. You will feel perpetually lifted and everything just naturally shines its radiant orgasmic nature. You become a naturally walking, breathing orgasmic infinite being of love through everything.

CHAPTER 20

MIRROR REFLECTION TECHNIQUE

TO KEEP YOU ON THE ORGASMIC VIBRATION

The mirror reflection technique is simply whatever you see in another is what has to be somewhere inside of yourself. A running program, a memory, though it may be hidden so deep, through the illusion that it seems it has nothing to do with you. However from my own experience I know the reflection is inside myself, and you will find that too when you become aware to notice it.

It is the trickiest part of evolving to higher vibrations because of the denial and habitual ways we have reacted for so many years, throughout the years until mastering it. And mastering may take some time because getting out of this old habit can take consistent daily work. The best way to know you have mastered it is when you see the best in everyone and every situation and experience. So the reflection is always simple to see once we let go of our own denial that we could not possibility have such negative programs, but we do. It seems to be inherited in our birth upon the physical plane in physical embodiment. Our purpose can be to realize this through reflection until we ace it eventually, bit by bit.

Just as a mirror will only give us our own reflection back can be seen the same way with what we see in everything and everyone else regardless of what are old denial beliefs have dictated to us previously. It takes a real dedicated passion to work on mastering to realize what we experience we get back because what we experience is already in us to work through to finally delete the old beliefs.

What else could all of the negative programs that we react with be there for? Like fear, hate, anger, revenge, separation, blame, pessimism and any other lower vibration, they are all there for a beneficial orgasmic reason. It must be for the reason to finally let go of by evolving past those not so good feeling attitudes. The only reason that we feel any pleasure from them is because it has a memory associated with pleasure to be angry or revengeful to begin with. If we don't work on them we will stay stuck in life time after lifetime until we remember what they are there for and work on evolving all reflections we don't want into the higher energy.

This is the reason I love the mirror reflection technique and have been using it for over 20 years because it has so much power once you get over the edge of denial and see it for its highest opportunity of benefits for our self.

So big congrats to you if you have already been using the mirror reflection technique and have come to realize the amazing power of it through evolving into higher consciousness. If you have not yet, then bit by bit you will also notice quite a difference in your state of being eventually.

It takes consistent practice repetitiously to create the highest memories from infinite consciousness and is always worth it.

All you have to do is have your invisible mirror with you all the time and take the time to pause in any reflection that you don't like and continue to perceive it differently with a high vibration. Then take notice how great you feel after. Also you will take more notice too of mirror reflections of your experiences that reflect orgasmic vibrations of experiences too. It will be the most fantastic way to keep yourself on track daily to keep orgasmic living to expand until it becomes the only way you choose to live, always orgasmically.

\` \` \` \` \` \` \` \` \` \` \` \` \` \` \` \` \` \` \`

ORGASMIC QUOTES, NEW WORDS AND AFFIRMATIONS SPICED WITH A COUPLE ORGASMIC POEMS

MY ORGASMIC QUOTES

" Orgasm is the hidden key to unlocking the door to Infinity"

" To live life in the most orgasmic ways is living Heaven on Earth."

"Orgasm can show us how to be our own authority by the feeling it give us to expand into our daily life when we stay aware."

"Orgasm shines the light through the fog to other dimensions showing us there's more then just being physical into the journey of infinite realities."

"You can experience orgasmic bliss when doing normal chores, like taking out the garbage, change your perception and it will change everything."

"The wild ride of orgasm is all inside, it leaves such an impression that it entices us forever wanting more, expanding our consciousness into the infinite void from once we came and then to experience orgasmic living in physical. Being wise in our experiences of living life orgasmically."

"What a genius Creator to create the hidden key through orgasm to one day unlock universal gems of wisdom. Enticing our desire to find heaven in a place so few dared to realize, orgasm being the key to unlocking the door into the gap of heavenly bliss, the state of our natural being, where the genuine ultimate power is that connects us to the Infinite Creator."

"Orgasm so ecstatically shows us that the feelings of bliss or heaven and love are of the highest vibrational heart feelings of pleasure and the sparks to get us to expand into more of what the future can offer us."

\ \ \ \ \ \ \ \ \ \ \ \ \ \ \ \ \ \ \

NEW WORDS

For anyone new to creating new words, it is a teaching from Ramtha's channeled by J. Z. Knight.

When we experience a feeling that our normal words is not able to specifically describe to define our experience, we create a new word.

The new word is more describable because it is created in the powerful present moment that I experience the emotion that then is fueled through my heart that transforms into a feeling.

Using our creative orgasmic state of being to its full potential by creating the new word to describe what that feeling is. This is a list of new words I did create while writing this book, as I felt it and allowed it to release to come out verbally.

Zamactrifying, ... orgasmically ...ecstatical ...

lumpiously orgnicimis ... expinluminsusary.

Affirmations for the Infinite Orgasmic Manifestor

I have added affirmations that you may use and find helpful as you evolve into the Infinite You, the Infinite Orgasmic Manifestor. You are probably already aware of how powerful affirmations can be in the beginning of anything we desire to change. Affirmations give us that reminder to change from the limited old programs that so automatically keep running in are minds. The reason is because we need that kind of leverage when we want to outgrow our old limitations of beliefs into expanding potential unlimited beliefs that become our knowing. Just by repeating the affirmations before sleep or upon awakening or in a trance like state, anytime the reminders are needed.

You can record the affirmations as you read them in your voice verbally and listen to them with your own preference of soft playing background music. The best time to play them or read them is when you are in a trance like state and for most this is just before sleep or upon awakening or when you are just dazing. The reason affirmations work this way is because our consciousness mind is less active and allows our subconscious to pick up on the affirmations without any resistance. Affirmations are always in the present tense because that's how they are the most affective, as you read them you are affirming I AM to yourself. The I Am is so powerful and eventually will merge your ego personality with infinite spirit through repetition.

Affirmations for the Infinite You and for your Highest Potential

- *I am a infinite creator creating all of my reality, this is my passionate purpose in my journey in this physical plane of existence*
- *I am connected to the Infinite Source of All That Is…I have merged my ego personality with Infinite Source and I am an extension of the Infinite*
- *Nothing alters my orgasmic bliss feelings that I experience all day long because staying in the high vibration frequency of bliss and peace allows everything to be of the highest benefit for me and all others and every situation and experience*
- *Since I am love, I love myself and love flows outward into everyone and everything*
- *I know I am worth all that I desire because I am connected to the Infinite Source, I honor that in my being and celebrate it daily*
- *I am powerful as I am connected to the Infinite and activated my Infinite Gene in my body's DNA*
- *I feel and experiences all the greatest harmonious benefits of orgasmic bliss, living it daily, I am healthy and sustain my health, I am light in thoughts and embodiment, I am creative and express my creativity*

- *I see everything as opportunity for me to evolve and expand bit by bit into the Infinite Creator I am, co-creating with the Infinite Source*
- *My appearance is youthful because I am using less time in space, living life through love which sustains my blissful feelings and experiences, it sustains my youthfulness in my attitude and appearance*
- *I radiate and shine of my love and orgasmic bliss magnetism and I see it in everyone I encounter*
- *I am outrageous, adventurous, courageous and live my life to the fullest every day*
- *I am accepting and allowing of all others as I know they are on their own journey*
- *Whenever I see a reflection that does not resonate with me, that I am not accepting I turn to myself and know what I need to work on and it brings me back to my high vibration*
- *I have a great sense of humor and see the joy in everything and everyone, smiling is my natural result of my joy, fun and excitement of life*
- *Transforming all challenges to opportunities of orgasmic bliss comes easily and natural to me, it is all an opportunity to get back to my high energy state of being*
- *I feel lighter and better then ever, I am in great shape physically, energetically and spiritually…*
- *I see my reflection in everyone and everything*
- *Though I am unique in my journey I know I am a part of the whole*
- *I know what I put out always comes back to me, so I always put out the best of the highest vibration*
- *I easily relax and focus in bringing my bliss into my alignment with Infinite Source*
- *I have mastered focusing, imagining or meditating so easily now, I experience my desires manifested so quick and simply now by*

giving it some thought and feelings, and let it go in trust and see the results quickly

- *Love, joy, passion, empathy, laughter, fun, excitement, bliss is a natural for me, it has become habitual from practicing, I have mastered it and it keeps me on a high vibration*
- *I know that everything is possible, if I can think it then it can be*
- *Any disharmony in my thoughts or body allows me to simply and quickly bring me back into harmony and sustains my perfect health*
- *I am aware and listen to the resonating feelings of my blissful heart and follow my hearts path*
- *I see everything so clearly, my eye sight is perfect*
- *I learn, expand and evolve from every experience I go through and perpetually create the greatest ease and highest benefits of every experience. I am all possibility, I am an Infinite Creator creating all of my reality and I honor it.*

These are just a few affirmations to get you started, you can expand on each one or add to the list to personalize it for more specifics too. It is all up to you, whatever you desire just put it into an affirmation in the present tense with I AM and through repetition of even a couple weeks I know you will find an amazing difference.

ORGASMIC POEMS

ORGASM SHOWS THE WAY

So expanded relaxed in the flow
Of sensual pleasure caressing me so
Into a world of pure ecstasy
My body is trembling like bliss has finally found me

The journey to get to the one final point
Prepping, seducing through every single thought
Leading up to the moment to release
Then just as I let go the feeling in extreme envelopes me

Into a magical space in time
Where nothing else matter but this feeling so mine
Taking me deep into a void so free
Everything pulsing, contracting, electrical currents sparking
Into a magical release of heavens blissful experience

This surely must be showing me heaven
Though only for such a short moment in time
Leaving me wanting more of this magnificence
The message became so clearly defined

This is a taste of heavenly bliss in the most ecstatic state
To feel it is to know it to own it forever

Like rolling in sparkling magical dust
Sparking every bodily nerve to ignite to implode
Into the void of eternity as a reminder of what we can be forever more

When we expand our self to curiosity
To look into the future world filled through luminosity
Of what we will become in our Divine Blossoming
Just from the tantalizing spiral of heavenly orgasm's bliss

KEY TO BLISS OUR NATURAL DESTINY

Oh blessed blissful orgasm take me away
Into the place where I love to stay
Heavenly state with no thought or doubts
Just the basking in eternity's love
Where limited descriptions won't be found
Just the blossoming of forever's map we will be the echoing crown

Attachments of what I thought love was is no longer true
Love has nothing to do with all I once thought and valued to be true
Limits have been blown away to never return
Now that I have basked in ecstasy of orgasm home
The paradise all along has always been there to know
Not for a few moments but forever to grow

All unseen things have the most powerful states
The wind is a non thing yet shows itself with its force
and howling sounds it forsakes
Time also a non thing yet has enslave most to struggle
Bending it as much as humanly possible
Love a non thing yet humanity can twist into conditions
Into anything they want without knowing its true natures ambition
Heaven most long for
but it escapes them like grains of sand in their hands
Because all things invisibles are the most powerful to man

Orgasm is fleeting in the release of sexual acts
Yet it is the key to unlock the door from the past
To knowing the experience is a reminder of what could be
From just a moment of experiencing its power is intoxicating
Always to come back for more for us of what we can be

When orgasm is expanded into our daily lives
We find heaven in all we see and do just for its prize
Of the feelings that can sustain us throughout our days
When we come to know of orgasms maze
We bring heaven when we realize
That heaven is what we have just become
We are then heaven and love in our orgasmic self
And radiate it while we live in our paradise on earth
in physical orgasmic tantalized from all that we felt
We are the kingdom of heaven that orgasm has birthed

EXTENDED READING

Dan Winter:

http://www.danwinter.com

Information of our body's response to bliss and the benefits

Bruce Lipton:

http://www.brucelipton.com

Changing Our Body's DNA

I hope you enjoyed the adventure and that it will continue to lead you into the orgasmic journey of experiencing as much heavenly bliss on earth as you can. Which eventually can become all the time in this spacious journey in physical.

Infinitely AnnaMarie

Also by AnnaMarie Antoski

Infinite Manifesting
The Journey to Your Infinite Self

Evolving Reality of Bewitched
Living a Magical Life

Stumbling Through Infinity
Heart Reflection Poetry

Knowledge Transforms to Wisdom
Consciousness Expanding Poetry

Forever in Bloom
Poetry Collection

Soon to Be Released

The Self Healing Master in You

Disclaimer: No parts of this book or the author hold any responsibility for individual's own choices and decisions for medical assistance or medication

ABOUT THE AUTHOR

AnnaMarie Antoski has studied the nature of reality for over 20 years with consistent passion and has integrated what she has learned into her life experiences. Sharing her self healing and evolving psychic abilities she has become an inspiration in her field of experiences.

For more information

http://www.infinite-manifesting.org/

www.ingramcontent.com/pod-product-compliance
Lightning Source LLC
Chambersburg PA
CBHW020040040426
42331CB00030B/104

* 9 7 8 0 9 8 6 8 8 4 4 0 5 *